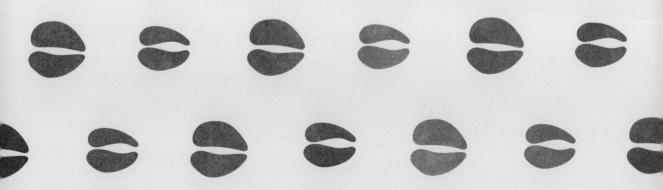

BISON
COMMUNITY BUILDERS AND GRASSLAND CARETAKERS

FRANCES BACKHOUSE

ORCA BOOK PUBLISHERS

The sun sets behind a bison standing on the open prairie in Badlands National Park.
JAMIE LAMB/GETTY IMAGES

Text copyright © Frances Backhouse 2025

Published in Canada and the United States in 2025 by Orca Book Publishers.
orcabook.com

All rights are reserved, including those for text and data mining, AI training and similar technologies. No part of this publication may be reproduced or transmitted in any form or by any means, electronic or mechanical, including photocopying, recording or by any information storage and retrieval system now known or to be invented, without permission in writing from the publisher. The publisher expressly prohibits the use of this work in connection with the development of any software program, including, without limitation, training a machine-learning or generative artificial intelligence (AI) system.

Library and Archives Canada Cataloguing in Publication
Title: Bison : community builders and grassland caretakers / Frances Backhouse.
Names: Backhouse, Frances, author.
Series: Orca wild ; 17.
Description: Series statement: Orca wild ; 17 | Includes bibliographical references and index.
Identifiers: Canadiana (print) 20240387368 | Canadiana (ebook) 20240387236 |
ISBN 9781459839236 (hardcover) | ISBN 9781459839243 (PDF) | ISBN 9781459839250 (EPUB)
Subjects: LCSH: American bison—Juvenile literature. | LCSH: American bison—Ecology—Juvenile literature. | LCSH: American bison—Conservation—Juvenile literature. | LCGFT: Informational works. | LCGFT: Instructional and educational works.
Classification: LCC QL737.U53 B33 2025 | DDC j599.64/3—dc23

Library of Congress Control Number: 2024939277

Summary: Part of the nonfiction Orca Wild series for middle-grade readers and illustrated with color photographs throughout, this book introduces kids to North American bison. It discusses bison history, habitat, biology and threats to survival, and how scientists, conservationists and young people are working to protect bison everywhere.

Orca Book Publishers is committed to reducing the consumption of nonrenewable resources in the production of our books. We make every effort to use materials that support a sustainable future.

Orca Book Publishers gratefully acknowledges the support for its publishing programs provided by the following agencies: the Government of Canada, the Canada Council for the Arts and the Province of British Columbia through the BC Arts Council and the Book Publishing Tax Credit.

The author and publisher have made every effort to ensure that the information in this book was correct at the time of publication. The author and publisher do not assume any liability for any loss, damage, or disruption caused by errors or omissions. Every effort has been made to trace copyright holders and to obtain their permission for the use of copyrighted material. The publisher apologizes for any errors or omissions and would be grateful if notified of any corrections that should be incorporated in future reprints or editions of this book.

Front cover photo by brentawp/iStock/Getty Images Plus.
Back cover photo by Peter Adams/Getty Images.
Author photo by Mark Zuehlke.
Design by Troy Cunningham.
Edited by Kirstie Hudson.

Printed and bound in South Korea.

"But when the buffalo went away the hearts of my people fell to the ground, and they could not lift them up again."
—Alaxchíia Ahú (Plenty Coups), chief of the Apsáalooke Nation, 1928

This book is dedicated to everyone who helped save the buffalo, and to all those who continue to welcome the buffalo back with uplifted hearts.

CONTENTS

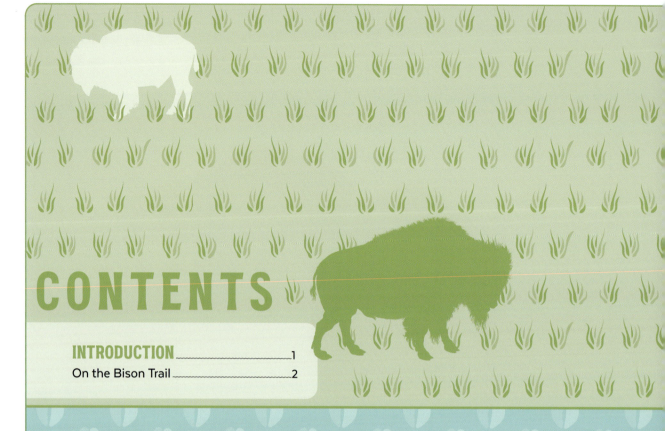

INTRODUCTION ... 1
On the Bison Trail ... 2

1. MEET THE HERD
Big and Burly ... 5
Hi, My Name Is _____ ... 6
Home, Home on the Range ... 7
Hairdos and Humps ... 9
Buffalo Belly Buttons ... 10
Safety In Numbers ... 11
Serious Play ... 13
Filling the Grass Tank ... 14
The Wonders of Bison Snot ... 15
Herd Life ... 16
Bellowing Battling Bulls ... 17
Winter Survival ... 19
The End of the Trail ... 21
Life Goes On ... 21

2. BETTER WITH BISON
Big Influencers ... 25
Setting the Table ... 26
Building Community ... 28
Plop! ... 29
Popular Poop ... 30
Rolling in the Dirt ... 30
Wallows Welcome All ... 32
Rub-a-Dub-Dub ... 33
Keeping Neighbors Cozy ... 34
Gardeners and Trailblazers ... 35
Food Trucks on Four Legs ... 36
The Circle of Life ... 37
Keeping Ecosystems Healthy and Strong ... 39

4. HOMECOMING

Atatíće?'s Dream	63
Founders	64
To the Rescue	65
Moo-ve Over, Buffalos	67
Stuffed, Mounted and Caged	68
The Dark Side of Success	69
Tears and Smiles	70
Survivors in the Wild	71
Wood Buffalo Woes	72
Double Whammy	73
Trouble in Yellowstone	74
Renewing Relationships	75
Look What's in That Wallow!	76
Bison Business	77
Preserving and Protecting	78
Letting Bison Be Bison	79
Safety Tips for Bison Watchers	81
Saluting Bison	82
Wise Words	83

3. THUNDER AND SILENCE

Incredible Numbers	43
Sharing the Land	44
Delicious and Nutritious	45
From Tongue to Tail	46
Getting the Upper Hand	48
Masters of Disguise	49
Luring the Herd	50
Pounds and Jumps	51
Teamwork	52
Hunters on Horseback	53
Musket Balls and Bullets	54
The Booming Bison Trade	55
Trainloads of Destruction	55
Killing for the Thrill	57
Support for the Slaughter	57
Nearly Gone	59

Glossary	86
Resources	87
Acknowledgments	88
Index	89

Bison exit a pen made of hay bales on the American Prairie nature reserve in 2005. These 16 bison were the founders of a herd that now numbers close to 1,000.
AMERICAN PRAIRIE

INTRODUCTION

When I was 12 my family moved from Montreal to Calgary. My father flew out first. My mother, sister, brother and I went a few weeks later by train. My favorite part of the journey was crossing the prairies. The wide skies and vast golden wheat fields were just like pictures I had seen in school textbooks. In my excitement I didn't realize what was missing. Anyone who traveled across the prairies 200 years earlier—before there was any thought of building a railroad there—would have seen great herds of bison all along the way. I saw none.

Things got very bad for bison in the 1800s, and they barely escaped extinction. In 1897 a few of Canada's last bison were taken to Banff National Park and placed in a fenced enclosure. Their descendants were still living in Banff when I moved west. They were my introduction to bison. Tourists could drive slowly through their paddock on a gravel road and marvel at the massive beasts. It only took about five minutes

to do the full loop. But if you rolled down the windows you could hear their grunting conversations and smell the dust they stirred up.

ON THE BISON TRAIL

Over the following years I saw bison now and then in other places. But they really came into focus when I went to Montana to visit a nature reserve called American Prairie. It was created to provide a home for bison and their grassland neighbors. A big home! The dream is that it will grow to stretch across 5,000 square miles (13,000 square kilometers) and give 5,000 bison enough room to roam without feeling hemmed in by fences.

The first 16 members of that future herd were trucked to the reserve in the fall of 2005. On a cold, sunny November afternoon, I stood with a small group of people who had come to watch the bison be released from their holding pen. Two teens were given the honor of opening the gate. When they got the signal, they swung it wide. I expected the bison to gallop out, but it was 20 minutes before the first one poked its nose past the gateposts. Then they all followed that brave leader out onto the open prairie. They were the first bison to set foot on this land in 120 years.

Since then I have been on the bison trail. As these amazing animals return to their former homelands, I am excited to have so many opportunities to get acquainted. At Old Man on His Back Prairie and Heritage Conservation Area in Saskatchewan, I watched them ramble across the rolling hills and laid my hand on a boulder that their ancestors rubbed smooth long ago. In Theodore Roosevelt National Park in North Dakota, I camped with bison.

This bison paid no attention to me as it walked past my campsite in Theodore Roosevelt National Park.
FRANCES BACKHOUSE

They sauntered right through the campground every day like they own the place, which of course they do. Those are just a couple of my bison adventures. I know others await me. Bison are back like never before, and some of the most exciting chapters in this **conservation** success story are being written right now.

A herd of bison mothers and calves on the move in Yellowstone National Park.
NEAL HERBERT/NPS

1
MEET THE HERD

BIG AND BURLY

Bison are huge! In fact, they are North America's largest land animal. Full-grown adult males weigh around 1,600 pounds (726 kilograms). The heaviest of these heavyweights tip the scales at 2,000 pounds (907 kilograms). That's as much as a small car or two grand pianos. Full-grown females weigh about 1,000 pounds (500 kilograms).

Male bison—known as bulls—measure 10 to 12.5 feet (3 to 3.8 meters) from nose to tail. Stand three of them in a line and their combined length is the same as a school bus. If you were in that bus, you could easily reach out the window and pat their high humped shoulders. The shoulder height of bulls ranges from 5.5 to 9 feet (1.7 to 2.7 meters). Females—or cows—are a bit shorter in both height and length.

Male bison are bigger than females and have wider heads, thicker horns, bushier head hair and bigger beards. A bull's shoulders are broader than his hips—like a football player in full gear. A cow's shoulders are narrower than her hips.

When a bison cow and bull stand side by side, it's easy to see that the bull is bigger and shaggier.
DESIGN PICS/PHILIPPE WIDLING/GETTY IMAGES

Those are impressive numbers, but there's more to bison than just being big and burly. They have a dramatic history, rich social lives and some awesome talents—like being able to pick their noses with their tongues! But before we explore all that, let's take a closer look at their name tag.

HI, MY NAME IS _____

When biologists talk about this **species** they usually refer to them as bison. Your neighbors might call them buffalo, and so might you. Both names are correct. One is a short form of their scientific name—*Bison bison*. The other goes way back to the time when Europeans first met them. Sometimes people say American bison or American buffalo to avoid confusing them with European bison, Asian water buffalo or African buffalo. Those distant relatives all belong to different species.

Much older names come from the languages of the many different Indigenous Peoples who have lived alongside these animals for tens of thousands of years. These include:

- aak'ii in Gwichya Gwich'in
- boy-zhan in Eastern Shoshone
- kuts in Paiute
- paskwâwimostos in Nēhiyawēwin
- paskwâw moshtosh in Northern Michif
- lii bufloo in Southern Michif
- tatanka in Lakota

As you'll see when you read on, I don't just stick to one name. I figure these beasts are big enough to wear a whole bunch of name tags.

HOME, HOME ON THE RANGE

Bison also have names that divide them into two groups based on their main *habitat*—the place where they live and can find everything they need to survive, including food, water and shelter. Plains bison spend most of their time in *grasslands* and other wide open country. Wood bison favor areas that have a mix of meadows for grazing and forests for protection from cold weather and predators. Plains bison and wood bison belong to the same species but different *subspecies*, or subgroups.

Before Europeans came to North America, plains bison roamed throughout most of what is now the United States, southwestern Canada and northern Mexico. The heart of their *range* was the *Great Plains*. This region stretches from the Mississippi River to the Rocky Mountains and from the middle of Alberta and Saskatchewan to southern Texas. Some plains bison also lived east of the Mississippi, south of the Great Plains and in valleys extending west into the Rocky Mountains.

The wood bison's original range included much of Alaska, Yukon, the Northwest Territories, northern Alberta and northern British Columbia, plus a bit of northern Saskatchewan. The two subspecies mostly kept apart from each other, but they occasionally crossed paths. These meetings usually happened in winter, when some wood bison wandered south and some plains bison drifted north.

ADAPTED FROM FIGURE 4. HISTORICAL (PRE-SETTLEMENT) DISTRIBUTION OF WOOD BISON AND PLAINS BISON IN NORTH AMERICA. COSEWIC ASSESSMENT AND STATUS REPORT 2013. CANADA.CA

ORIGINAL RANGE OF **BISON** IN **NORTH AMERICA**

WOOD BISON RANGE
PLAINS BISON RANGE
THE GREAT PLAINS

SPOT THE DIFFERENCE
PLAINS BISON and WOOD BISON

1 HEAD HAIR
PLAINS BISON: Thick and bushy.
WOOD BISON: Long wavy strands droop over forehead.

2 BEARD
PLAINS BISON: Long, dense and bell shaped.
WOOD BISON: Short, thin and pointed.

3 SHOULDER CAPE
PLAINS BISON: Long and thick. May hang below knees.
WOOD BISON: Lightweight. Doesn't hang below knees.

4 FRONT LEG HAIR
PLAINS BISON: Long and thick, especially behind the legs.
WOOD BISON: Short.

5 HUMP
PLAINS BISON: Rounded.
WOOD BISON: Sharply angled toward the head.

(TOP) JACOB W. FRANK/NPS; (BOTTOM) ©PARKS CANADA, WOOD BUFFALO NATIONAL PARK

HAIRDOS AND HUMPS

Wood bison are about 20 percent heavier and taller than plains bison. Their larger bodies help them cope with the North's extremely cold winters, and their longer legs are better for traveling through deep soft snow. But unless the two kinds of bison are standing side by side, most people need clues other than size to tell them apart. Start by checking out their beards and hairdos. A plains bison has a large, bell-shaped beard and a woolly mass of head hair that puffs out in all directions. A wood bison has a smaller, pointier beard and shorter head hair, which lays flatter and flops over its forehead.

The shagginess of the plains bison doesn't stop at its head. A thick cape of long hair drapes across its shoulders, hangs down from its neck and chest and wraps its front legs like baggy fur pants. This dark woolly coat covers only the front half of the body. The rest is covered with a smooth coat of short hair that is lighter brown. The contrast between front and back makes it look like the bison forgot to finish getting dressed.

A wood bison also wears a thicker, darker coat on the front half of its body, but the hair on its shoulders, neck, chest and front legs isn't as long and heavy as the plains bison's. On the other hand, the wood bison does have a longer tail with a bigger tassel.

Female bison—like this one—have shorter, thinner beards and less head hair than males. They also have smaller horns than males.
DIANE RENKIN/NPS

Another useful identification feature is the shape of the shoulder hump. A wood bison's hump is tall and triangular, and the highest point is well ahead of the front legs. A plains bison has a more rounded hump, with the highest point right above the front legs.

BUFFALO BELLY BUTTONS

Plains bison and wood bison look a little different from each other but lead similar lives. It all begins in spring, when they come into the world. Bison are born from late March to late June, depending on how long winter lasts where they live. On the northern Great Plains they are

Very young bison calves are nicknamed red dogs because of their reddish-orange coats.
NPS/JIM PEACO

born right when the prairie crocuses are blooming. The Cree name for these flowers is moostoos ohtsi—which translates as buffalo's belly button in English.

Newborn bison have strong survival instincts. Just minutes after they emerge, they start trying to stand. They may topple over a few times before making it up onto all four legs. But within 10 minutes they will take their first shaky steps. Two or three hours later these babies can scamper fast enough to keep up with their mother and the rest of the herd.

Young calves have short, fuzzy reddish-orange coats. The coat starts to turn dark brown at about three months old. By then a calf's shoulder hump is beginning to take shape, and stubby little horns have popped up on the top of its head. Calves weigh only 30 to 70 pounds (14 to 32 kilograms) at birth, but they grow quickly, gaining more than 2.2 pounds (1 kilogram) a day. At first their only food is their mother's milk. Over the summer they gradually shift to eating plants.

This bison calf's coat has started to change color, and its horns have started to grow. Its ears are very visible now but will nearly disappear as its head hair gets thicker.
NPS/ASHTON HOOKER

SAFETY IN NUMBERS

Bison mothers almost always have just one calf at a time. Twins are very rare. But young bison are never lonely because they are part of a close community—a herd made up of cows, calves and young bulls. All the cows in a herd give birth around the same time because every mother wants to give her baby the best chance of surviving. When predators come around, it's much safer to be in a crowd than to be the only calf in sight.

Wolves and grizzly bears are the bison's main predators. They mostly kill calves and one-year-olds. Occasionally

Two scenes from a bison hunt by a Yellowstone National Park wolf pack. The wolves worked hard to make a kill, but the bulls fended off their attacks and finally fled. Wolves often fail in their attempts to prey on bison.
DANIEL STAHLER/NPS

they manage to bring down older bison. Coyotes also kill calves now and then.

Calves can do little to protect themselves against these hunters, but adult bison have great anti-predator defenses. They can gouge and stab with their sharp horns. Those horns can also hook an enemy and send it flying. Their sharp hooves can strike hard blows. Their thick hide acts like armor, with the heavy hair on their head and the front part of their body adding extra protection. They can also run fast, leap high and quickly twist and turn by pivoting on their front feet. Even when they are standing still, their massive size is enough to make a predator think twice about attacking.

When predators do attack, adult bison usually stand their ground and face their foes head on. Older members

Bison are natural athletes. They can sprint at up to 35 miles (56 kilometers) an hour, and if they slow down a bit, they can run for many miles. They can jump vertically as high as 6 feet (1.8 meters) or 14 feet (4.3 meters) horizontally. They are also strong swimmers.

A bison uses its powerful legs to launch into a high jump.
PCHOUI/GETTY IMAGES

of a herd often gather around the junior members, with their heads lowered and their horns ready for action. They also work together to protect themselves and their companions. It's hard for a grizzly bear or pack of wolves to pick off one bison when they have furious defenders coming at them from every side.

SERIOUS PLAY

Bison moms and their babies stick close together at first. That's for security and so the calf can nurse whenever it's hungry. If they get separated, they call to each other until they are reunited. Mothers beckon with low-pitched grunts. Calves reply with high-pitched grunts and bleats. But calves need to learn to take care of themselves. With each passing week they venture farther from their mothers and stay away longer. Usually they hang around with other calves.

Two bison calves test their strength with a friendly tussle.
TROY HARRISON/GETTY IMAGES

Playing is important work for growing bison. Running and frolicking build their muscles to make them stronger and faster. Chasing and dodging each other are skills they need in order to avoid ending up in a predator's belly. And butting heads with buddies is valuable training for male calves, who will someday compete with each other as adults. A calf's other important work is eating. Before winter comes, it needs to grow as big as possible and build up its energy reserves.

FILLING THE GRASS TANK

Eating is also a priority for the grown-ups. Bison mainly eat grasses and *sedges*, which are stiff-stemmed grasslike plants that grow in wet meadows. The animals move along like living lawn mowers, shearing off greenery with the wide row of cutting teeth that runs along the front of their lower jaw. When the grazing is good, all those mouthfuls add up to 15 to 30 pounds (7 to 14 kilograms) of food a day. Bison concentrate on gaining weight in spring and summer, when food is plentiful and easy to get at, because they are sure to lose weight in fall and winter, when plants die back and are buried by snow. The energy they store as fat fuels them when food is scarce. In fall and winter they also conserve energy by becoming less active, and their body chemistry changes so they don't need as much food.

To fill their grass tanks, bison graze for 9 to 11 hours every day. They also spend a lot of time *ruminating*, or chewing their cud. Bison have four stomachs and a complex digestion process that requires chewing all their food twice. The first round grinds up the plant material before it goes to their first stomach, where tiny **microbes** start breaking it down. Every so often the bison stops grazing and burps up a ball of partly digested food called the cud. Then it chews some more, mixing in plenty of saliva, and swallows again. Eventually the food passes through the other three stomachs for more digestion. Then the bison poops out what's left.

A bison's low-hanging head allows it to graze for hours without straining its neck.
BDPHOTO/GETTY IMAGES

THE WONDERS OF BISON SNOT

A bison's enormous first stomach can hold about 40 gallons (151 liters) of partly digested food. Every ounce of the soggy mash contains tens of millions of microbes (one million per milliliter). Without them, bison couldn't digest their food and would starve to death.

The microbes come from outside the bison's body. They end up inside through some clever tongue action. When bison

When a bison cleans its nose with its tongue, you can see the pink underside. The top of the tongue is black.
ERIC JOHNSTON/NPS

amble along with their heads low to the ground, they are constantly snuffling up dust and microbes, which then get stuck in their snot. If you watch a bison for a while you will probably catch it in the act of cleaning its nose. Its long tongue slips out of its mouth and reaches up to quickly probe each nostril. It returns to the bison's mouth with a load of mucus and microbes. The bison swallows, and everything goes straight to its stomach.

HERD LIFE

A one-year-old bison is called a yearling. It's not quite an adult yet, but it no longer needs or gets any attention from its mother. That's good, because by then she's usually busy looking after a new calf. Most female bison become mothers themselves for the first time when they are three or four years old. They spend their entire lives living in herds with other cows and their offspring. Cow herds range in size from a dozen or so bison to more than 100. They are led by older cows. These grandmothers and great-grandmothers have learned many life lessons that help keep the rest of the herd safe and healthy.

Male bison stay with the cows for their first three years. Then they join the big boys in smaller all-bull herds. As males get older they spend less and less time with other bison. The oldest bulls usually avoid company for most of the year.

Plains bison herds are usually bigger than wood bison herds. But the size of all herds changes often as different bison come together and drift apart. The biggest gatherings happen during the summer breeding season. This is the only time of year when mature bulls and cows mingle—and it's an exciting time to watch bison. While the calves race around and kick up their heels, the bulls act tough and compete for mates.

BELLOWING BATTLING BULLS

When bison bulls fight, their weapons are their heads and horns. Mostly they just shove each other head-to-head and grapple with locked horns. They might also deliver a few jabs with the pointed tips. But occasionally fights heat up. Then the opponents charge at each other and slam their heads together with so much force that one of them might somersault backward. Their slashing horns chop off

A fight between bison bulls in the breeding season is a noisy and dusty spectacle.
NPS

clumps of head hair and fling it about. But their hard skulls and the thick hair that covers their foreheads keep them from bashing each other's brains in. When they aren't smashing heads, they dance around each other like boxers and look for a chance to punch or stab. A well-placed blow can break ribs or make a deep gash.

The sound of a bellowing bison bull can be heard from miles away.
NEAL HERBERT/NPS

The biggest, fittest bulls almost always win breeding-season competitions. But winners and losers both pay a high cost. Bulls lose 10 to 15 percent of their body weight over the summer—an average of 200 pounds (91 kilograms). That's because mating contests take so much energy and distract bulls from grazing.

During the breeding season bulls spend most of their time trying to keep other bulls away from the cows they want to mate with. Physical combat is dangerous and exhausting. So whenever possible, bulls use body language and their voices to avoid getting into fights. They usually start with displays that are meant to intimidate. They paw the ground and fill the air with rowdy bellows that sound like a rumbling roar. Now and then they pause to pee on the ground and roll around in the dampened dirt. That might seem like a bizarre way to try to scare rivals, but smells in the bull's urine send important signals to other bison.

If neither bull is willing to back down, they both turn up the volume on their bellowing and draw closer. With every step, they snort and stamp their hooves down hard. They may lower their heads, but their tails will be raised high. Sometimes they strike a sideways pose to show off their size. Their posturing continues until one of the competitors retreats or a full-blown fight breaks out.

WINTER SURVIVAL

After the breeding season, the cows and mature bulls go back to leading separate lives. They spend the fall packing on a few last pounds and growing their thick winter coats. Bison have two layers of hair—a dense woolly undercoat and a top layer of long guard hairs. The guard hairs shed rainwater and frost to keep the fur below dry. The woolly layer underneath provides insulation against freezing temperatures and icy winds.

Two other essential parts of the bison winter survival kit are the head and hump.

A snow-covered bison stays cozy inside its thick winter coat. The woolly layer provides such good insulation that no body heat escapes to melt the snow.
NEAL HERBERT/NPS

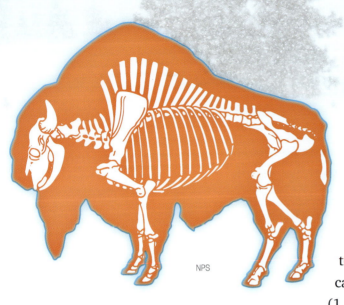

NPS

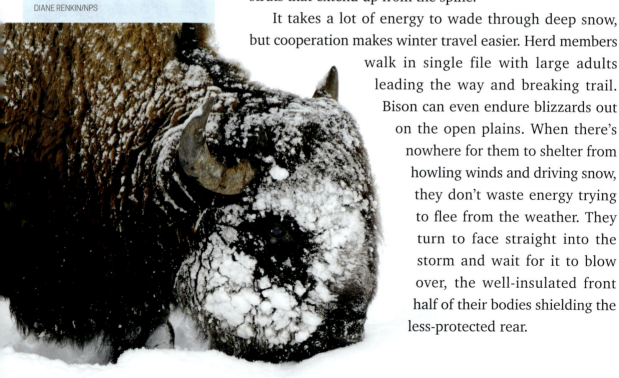

A bison stands in chest-deep snow and uses its head to dig down to buried food.
DIANE RENKIN/NPS

The plants that keep bison going through winter are often buried by snow for months. To reach them, bison swing their huge low-hanging heads from side to side to clear out feeding craters. They can shovel down through as much as 4 feet (1.2 meters) of snow. If you tried to use your head as a snowplow, it would be a real pain in the neck. Bison can do this with ease because of what's inside their humps—massive shoulder muscles supported by long struts that extend up from the spine.

It takes a lot of energy to wade through deep snow, but cooperation makes winter travel easier. Herd members walk in single file with large adults leading the way and breaking trail. Bison can even endure blizzards out on the open plains. When there's nowhere for them to shelter from howling winds and driving snow, they don't waste energy trying to flee from the weather. They turn to face straight into the storm and wait for it to blow over, the well-insulated front half of their bodies shielding the less-protected rear.

THE END OF THE TRAIL

Even with all these ways of coping, winter is still the deadliest season for bison. It's especially hard on calves. They are smaller and weaker than adults and have half as much body fat.

But bison of all ages struggle when winter is extra long or cold or snowy. The food they need to stay warm and power their bodies is hard to find. And if a bad winter follows a dry summer, they may not have enough fat reserves to carry them through to spring. A bison's risk of getting killed by wolves also increases as winter wears on and the snow piles up.

Other less-common causes of death include accidents and old age. When bison cross frozen rivers or lakes, they sometimes break through the ice and drown. Mature bulls occasionally die from injuries received during breeding-season fights. And when bison get very old, their teeth become so worn that they can no longer chew plants into small-enough pieces for proper digestion. In captivity bison can live 40 years or more. Their life span in the wild is usually about 10 to 20 years. Some cows in wild herds make it past 20 years. Bulls rarely reach that age.

LIFE GOES ON

After the hardships of winter, spring brings relief and renewal for bison. As the weather warms up, they shed their heavy winter coats and feast on fresh green grass shoots. Soon a new crop of calves will be born. If bison were partyers, I bet they would throw a big bash to celebrate this season—and many of their neighbors would join in to celebrate the bison. Having healthy herds of these special animals around is good for their whole community.

Nakoda student Armin Eashappie crushes a plant sample in a lab at the Canadian Light Source research center.
SHERRY BELLEGARDE

SHINING A LIGHT ON BISON

Kaleya Blackbird-Runns is from Carry the Kettle Nakoda Nation in Saskatchewan. The Nakoda have a close relationship with buffalo, but Kaleya didn't know much about these animals until she was 15. That was when she moved to Carry the Kettle and got involved in a unique school project.

One September day Kaleya and five classmates visited the community buffalo pasture with their teachers. Kaleya had never seen buffalo up close. They were much bigger than she expected. Keeping their distance from the herd, the students collected samples of food plants, soil and fallen hair.

A week later they traveled to the Canadian Light Source research center in Saskatoon to analyze their samples with Canada's only synchrotron. This gigantic machine produces extremely bright light and shoots it along narrow tubes to beamline stations. Researchers use the light to learn about the chemistry and invisible structure of all kinds of materials. Kaleya was excited about working with a machine that NASA—the United States National Aeronautics and Space Administration—uses to study asteroids.

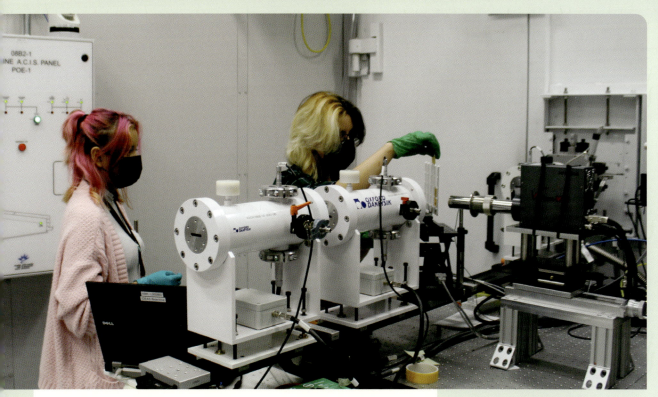

Kaleya Blackbird-Runns (left) and Armin Eashappie (right) work together at a synchrotron beamline station.
CANADIAN LIGHT SOURCE INC.

Guided by research center scientists, the students began by making 17 slides. Each small plastic square contained a plant, soil or hair sample. Then they took turns operating the beamline. One student put the slide in place. Another pushed the buttons that would light up the slide after they were safely out of the room. Everyone watched the action on big screens next door. Within seconds they could see graphs of the sample's chemistry.

During the project the students got to handle a buffalo hide, which turned out to be surprisingly heavy. Kaleya thought the hair on some parts felt weirdly like broom bristles while other parts were soft. They also learned from Elders about Nakoda traditions and teachings, including how buffalo agreed to sacrifice themselves to feed and take care of the Nakoda at the time of creation. "That's why we have so much respect for these animals," Kaleya says.

> "DOING THE BUFFALO PROJECT BROUGHT ME CLOSER TO MY IDENTITY AND WHO I AM. I'M VERY GRATEFUL FOR THAT."
>
> —KALEYA BLACKBIRD-RUNNS

Bison and prairie dogs are naturally good neighbors. Bison enjoy rolling in the loose dirt around prairie dog burrows. And prairie dogs like how grazing by bison keeps the grass around their doorways short.
MARK NEWMAN/GETTY IMAGES

2
BETTER WITH BISON

BIG INFLUENCERS

Have you ever met someone who is always doing things for others and whose many small actions make the world a better place? Bison are like that. I'm sure they don't know how great an impact they have, but that doesn't make it any less important. So who benefits from having bison around? Birds and butterflies. **Pronghorns** and prairie dogs. Wolves and wild licorice. Toads, jackrabbits and a whole lot more. Bison—especially plains bison—affect the lives of almost every animal and plant they cross paths with. Their influence is huge, just like them. And that outsized influence makes them a *keystone species*.

In an arch made of stone blocks, the keystone is the top block. It holds the other blocks in place and makes the arch strong. Pull out the keystone, and the arch collapses. A keystone species plays a similar role in the natural world. It supports other species and strengthens

Four pronghorns graze alongside a bison herd in Yellowstone National Park. Pronghorns live mainly on the Great Plains and happily share habitat with bison.
DIANE RENKIN/NPS

the whole community, or *ecosystem*. Remove a keystone species from the place where it belongs, and the ecosystem falls apart. Bison earn their keystone-species badge in many different ways. Eating tops the list. All animals eat, of course. But few of them have the bison's grazing style and enormous appetite for grasses.

SETTING THE TABLE

As a bison munches, it gently swings its head from side to side. This action creates a small area of short grass called a grazing patch. Every few minutes the bison takes several steps and starts munching again—creating patch after patch. Other herd members are doing the same thing nearby. Together they often create larger patches called grazing lawns.

Bison never stay in one place for long. If they did, they would run out of food. Instead they meander across the landscape, mowing as they go. After they move on, the grass sprouts back up. The grazed areas end up producing more grass during the growing season than ungrazed areas. And the new shoots are more tender and nutritious than the older grass. Every few weeks bison return to their favorite feeding areas to feast on the fresh greenery.

Grasses are the most obvious plants in a grassland, but mixed in with them are other plants with wide leaves and showy blooms. Bison mainly graze on grasses and sedges, and shun leafy flowering plants. That gives those plants a boost because they get more sunlight and room to grow when bison chomp down the grasses around them. And giving the leafy flowering plants a boost sets the table for many other animals. In these community dining rooms, butterflies sip nectar from the flowers and bees collect pollen. Pronghorns, deer, hares and rabbits nibble on leaves and stems. Mice and voles harvest seeds. And pocket gophers and moles devour the thick roots of plants such as wild licorice and prairie turnip.

> Bison usually walk about two to five miles (three to eight kilometers) a day. Occasionally they cover much greater distances. Cows tend to travel more than bulls because their herds are bigger, with more mouths to feed.

A male bison walks behind a female with a calf keeping pace beside them. Adult bulls like this one only hang around with cows and calves during the breeding season.
JACK-SOOKSAN/GETTY IMAGES

Plains spadefoot toads spend most of the year in underground burrows. They emerge during spring and summer rains to breed and lay their eggs in temporary pools of rainwater.
NPS

BUILDING COMMUNITY

Bison grazing lawns are also dance floors where male grouse gather to stomp their feet and show off to females in spring. And they are top-notch neighborhoods for prairie dogs and ground squirrels. These small rodents don't like tall grass growing around their homes because it blocks their view. Their safety depends on being able to spot enemies before they get close and being able to see each other to share danger warnings. Bison help them keep their lawns trimmed to the length they like.

Assisting these burrowers also builds up the broader community. Like bison, prairie dogs and ground squirrels are keystone species. Their special skill is digging underground tunnels that provide secondhand homes and hideouts for animals such as burrowing owls, tiger salamanders, black-footed ferrets and rattlesnakes. Ground squirrels and prairie dogs are also important prey for a wide range of predators, including black-footed ferrets, snakes, hawks, eagles, coyotes, badgers, foxes and bobcats.

It's spring, and these male sharp-tailed grouse are fancy-dancing to attract mates. The short grass of a bison grazing lawn is ideal for their performance. Later the females will nest in nearby places with shrubs and longer grass.
NPS

PLOP!

When bison eat, they don't just take. They also give back—big-time! The average bison produces 10 to 12 quarts (9.5 to 11 liters) of poop and many gallons of pee (no one has measured exactly how much) every day. Since bison are always on the move, they spread all this fantastic fertilizer far and wide. It feeds the plants that feed the bison. It also feeds plants that provide food and shelter for many other animals.

The poop plops out as Frisbee-sized patties that start drawing a crowd the moment they land. The first to arrive are poop-loving flies that quickly lay their eggs in the soft, moist mound before it begins to dry and harden. Dung beetles start showing up a few hours later, once a crust has formed on the outside. As you may know, dung is another word for poop. Dung beetles are poop specialists. When their eggs hatch, the *larvae* eat the dung. Once things get going, you can find more than 1,000 adult dung beetles of many different kinds in and on a single bison patty. Some species lay their eggs right in the poop. Others make tiny dung balls to hold their eggs. Then they either roll the balls away and leave them on the ground or bury them in tunnels.

Soon other bugs come to eat the eggs and larvae of the early arrivals. Ants often settle in for a longer stay. Over time each patty pumps up the local insect population. And more insects means more food for birds, bats, lizards, toads, spiders and other insect eaters.

Two dung beetles roll a ball of dung across the ground.
JOE BRUCE/NPS

Plants sprouting in and around an old bison patty get plenty of fertilizer to boost their growth.
FRANCES BACKHOUSE

POPULAR POOP

The usefulness of bison poop doesn't end there. When ground squirrels and prairie dogs can't find enough fresh food in early spring, they eat bison patties as emergency rations. They may not taste terrific, but they're full of undigested bits of plants that provide some nutrition.

For burrowing owls, bison patties are perfect for home improvements. These little owls often scatter scraps of dried dung around their burrow entrances and in the tunnels that lead to their nesting chambers. It attracts dung beetles, which burrowing owls like to eat. The decorations also tell other burrowing owls that a burrow has been claimed.

Toads and snakes sometimes crawl under old bison patties that have softened on the bottom but are still hard on top. It's a good way to get out of the sun or rain and hide from predators. These little huts are also well stocked with insects, earthworms and other tasty snacks.

ROLLING IN THE DIRT

Another way bison shape their environment is by wallowing. A bison *wallow* is a shallow circular or oval pit where bison roll around—or wallow—in the dirt. (*Wallow* is one of those funny words that names both a thing and an action.)

Wallows are started by bulls during breeding-season face-offs. The bulls paw the ground with their hooves and tear at it with their horns, uprooting plants and baring the soil. They also regularly drop to the ground and wallow in the wallow. As they throw their heavy bodies back and forth, they pack down the earth and stir up great clouds of dust.

Dust billows around a wallowing bison that has rolled right onto its back.
NPS

Over time wallows often grow to be as large as 10 to 13 feet (3 to 4 meters) wide and a foot (30 centimeters) deep in the middle.

Once a wallow is created, any bison may use it—and all bison love to wallow. Bulls are the only ones that wallow to intimidate and impress rivals, but there are several other good reasons for rolling around in the dirt. Wallowing helps bison get rid of their woolly winter hair. It also scratches itchy body parts that they can't reach with their hooves. And it's great for itch prevention, because the powdery soil that gets worked into the wallower's coat smothers lice and other biting bugs. In summer a dusty coat also helps bison beat the heat, and wallows are a pleasant place to lie because the bare dirt is cooler than the grass.

This bison calf has already learned that a dusty wallow is a pleasant place to rest on a hot summer day.
NPS

Bison use wallows over and over, year after year, so they last a long time. A calf could easily take its first dust bath in a wallow that its great-grandfather started.

WALLOWS WELCOME ALL

Bison wallows are an important resource for their community, especially in dry environments. In spring and early summer, these bowls of packed earth collect snowmelt and rainwater. The biggest and deepest wallows may hold the water for weeks before it soaks away into the soil or evaporates.

While the small pools last, many animals drop by to drink from them. Swallows also swoop down to pick up mud for nest building. Toads, frogs, turtles and insects come to paddle about or lay their eggs. And plants enthusiastically suck up the extra moisture in the soil in and around the wallows. Their lush greenery draws all kinds of plant eaters, and their flowers entice bees, butterflies and hummingbirds. These busy spots also attract predators of every sort.

A man sits at the edge of an old bison wallow in Kansas in 1897.
WILLARD DRAKE JOHNSON/
U.S. GEOLOGICAL SURVEY

In the bison's heyday there may have been more than 1.5 billion wallows on the Great Plains. Very old wallows can still be seen in some places where bison have been absent for more than a century. That's because the wallows still collect moisture and grow different plants than the drier areas around them.

A white-tailed jackrabbit stretches out in a bison wallow and relaxes after taking a vigorous dust bath.
JOHANE JANELLE

Once the ground dries up, pronghorns and rabbits sometimes tuck down into wallows to get out of the wind or hide from predators. Many birds and mammals also enjoy dust bathing in wallows. They just have to wait until the bison are out of the way so they don't get squashed.

RUB-A-DUB-DUB

Bison also scratch their itches and get rid of unwanted winter hair by rubbing against things while standing up. On the Great Plains they often use big boulders that were scattered across the land long ago by melting glaciers. These boulders are set so solidly into the ground that they don't budge no matter how hard bison push against them. Bison return to their favorite rubbing stones again

A bison bull rubs its forehead on a slender tree trunk. Missing bark and yellow splotches of dried sap show that this tree has been a popular rubbing post for a while.
JACOB W. FRANK/NPS

and again. Many have been used for thousands of years and visited by millions of bison. Their surfaces are worn smooth. The ground around them is grooved by the countless hooves that have trod there.

Rubbing stones create habitat for snakes and lizards. When bison trample the plants around the base of the stone, they form a lovely lounging patio for these cold-blooded reptiles. The snakes and lizards lie on the warm ground while the boulder blocks the wind and radiates heat absorbed from the sun.

When bison use trees as rubbing posts, the trees take a beating, but species that depend on grasslands or meadows benefit. That's because repeated rubbing kills some of the trees and keeps these open areas from turning into woodlands. The sweet sap that drips from broken branches and ripped bark is also a high-energy treat for various insects, birds and mammals.

KEEPING NEIGHBORS COZY

When the weather starts to warm up in spring, bison can't wait to throw off their heavy coats. Depending on where you live, you might feel the same way. But while you probably just shove your parka in a closet, bison drop their winter hair all over the countryside. Lots of their neighbors are happy to pick it up and recycle it.

Many kinds of birds like to weave bison hair into their nests. The woolly hair is soft, warm and water-repellent—perfect for cradling delicate eggs and snuggling baby chicks. It also smells strongly of bison. That's a bonus for the birds because it hides their own scent from predators that hunt with their noses, such as coyotes.

Bison supply plenty of this prized building material during the nesting season. A single bull sheds enough hair every year to meet the needs of more than 1,500 birds. Prairie dogs and ground squirrels also grab some of that hair. They gather big mouthfuls and carry them underground to line their dens and keep their pups comfortable.

GARDENERS AND TRAILBLAZERS

Bison even assist other species just by walking around. In spring, summer and fall, seeds get caught in their coats and hitch rides to new growing sites. The seeds may travel far before they fall to the ground or get left with a clump of hair in a wallow or by a rubbing stone.

With every footstep, bison create great sprouting spots. Each of their hooves covers about 12 square inches (77 square centimeters) of ground. That's the size of a large doughnut. Those hooves also carry a lot of weight. Their sharp outer edges break up the hard ground, making crevices that seeds and water can slip into. And the center of the hoof presses seeds into the soil, planting them like a gardener would.

In winter, bison are trailblazers. With their big bodies and habit of traveling in single file, they can plow through thick blankets of snow and tall drifts.

A mother ground squirrel pauses as she carries a mouthful of bison hair back to her burrow.
JOHANE JANELLE

This bison cow is decorated with hundreds of tiny green seed pods that got caught on her fur as she grazed. Eventually they will fall off, and some will sprout.
JOHANE JANELLE

Those obstacles can bring animals such as pronghorns to a standstill, so they like to follow bison trails when traveling through deep snow.

Bison feeding craters also make winter life easier for other members of their community. Once the bison have eaten and moved on, pronghorns and deer come to eat the plants they ignored. Birds that feed on the ground, such as grouse and horned larks, can find seeds in the cleared patches. And bison craters and tracks are great places for birds to take cover when winter winds are blowing hard.

Bison make their way through deep snow along a trail plowed out by the herd's leaders.
JIM PEACO/NPS

FOOD TRUCKS ON FOUR LEGS

Buffalo birds have a special relationship with bison. Nowadays they are better known as cowbirds, but I prefer their old name. After all, they buddied up to bison long before Europeans brought beef and dairy cows to North America. As bison walk and graze, these small birds walk along with them, staying close to their companions' noses and front feet. A bison's beard and hooves constantly disturb insects and send them leaping or flying. The birds snatch them as quickly as they appear. Buffalo birds will also perch on a bison's back or head and pick insects from its hair.

Bison herds are like grocery stores for buffalo birds. The catch is that these grocery stores keep moving. That means the birds can't stay in one place long enough to build a nest and raise a family. They solve this problem by getting someone else to do that work for them. Buffalo birds sneakily lay their eggs in the nests of other species when those birds aren't watching. The stay-at-home birds often fall for this trick and look after the buffalo-bird eggs and chicks as if they were their own.

Bison usually don't seem to mind buffalo birds hanging around with them—not even when they drink their snot and drool. *What?* Buffalo birds drink bison snot? It's true, they do. When there is no handy source of drinking water, these birds sometimes quench their thirst by fluttering close to a bison's nose and swigging strands of mucus as they drip down. That's icky to us, but it's a smart way to stay hydrated in a dry environment.

A male brown-headed cowbird perches on a bison's back.
NEAL HERBERT/NPS

A female brown-headed cowbird hovers below a bison's head as it sips on drips from its nose and mouth.
RON DUDLEY

THE CIRCLE OF LIFE

Bison give their final gifts to their community after they die. One adult bison's body can become a banquet for many different diners. When predators kill bison, they eat first. *Scavengers* follow and take whatever is left. The cleanup crew may include wolves, grizzly bears, black bears, coyotes, foxes, cougars, lynx, bobcats, wolverines, badgers, skunks, ground squirrels, prairie dogs, ravens, magpies, vultures or eagles. The smallest scavengers are flies, beetles and other insects. Some of them also lay their eggs in the rotting flesh so their larvae will have a meal as soon as they hatch.

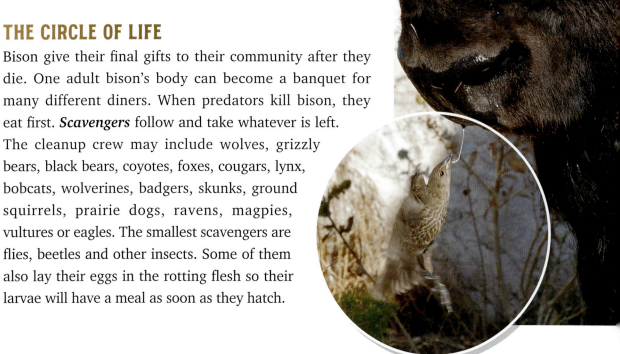

A coyote wades toward a dead bison lying in the Yellowstone River. Its approach has scared off the ravens and bald eagle that were feeding on the carcass.
JIM PEACO/NPS

Animals such as porcupines, mice and voles gnaw on bison bones to get the minerals they contain. Mice and voles also like to make their homes inside bison skulls, which offer excellent protection from predators and harsh weather. Ravens and hawks sometimes pick up a few long leg bones or ribs to add to the sticks they use for nest building. Other birds pluck hairs from the hide to line their nests.

Bit by bit the bison's massive carcass disappears. All the energy that was stored in its body spreads out into the bodies of other animals. Some of them are eaten in turn. Over time the energy also moves into the soil through the animals' droppings and their decaying bodies when they die. From there it feeds plants, and they eventually feed all kinds of plant eaters, including bison.

Bison horns are hollow and grow over a bony core that sticks out from the skull. They are made from the same material as your hair and fingernails.
SMITHSONIAN INSTITUTION ARCHIVES/CC0

As bison age, their shiny black horns become dull and gray. Bull horns get worn and blunted by years of tearing at the ground to make wallows. Older cows often have one horn that is just a stub because the curved part has broken off.

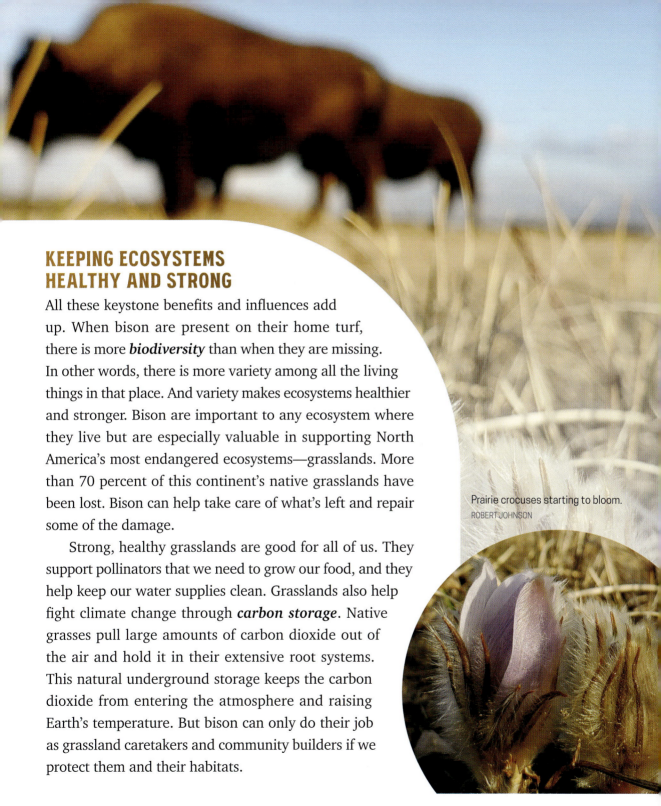

KEEPING ECOSYSTEMS HEALTHY AND STRONG

All these keystone benefits and influences add up. When bison are present on their home turf, there is more *biodiversity* than when they are missing. In other words, there is more variety among all the living things in that place. And variety makes ecosystems healthier and stronger. Bison are important to any ecosystem where they live but are especially valuable in supporting North America's most endangered ecosystems—grasslands. More than 70 percent of this continent's native grasslands have been lost. Bison can help take care of what's left and repair some of the damage.

Strong, healthy grasslands are good for all of us. They support pollinators that we need to grow our food, and they help keep our water supplies clean. Grasslands also help fight climate change through *carbon storage*. Native grasses pull large amounts of carbon dioxide out of the air and hold it in their extensive root systems. This natural underground storage keeps the carbon dioxide from entering the atmosphere and raising Earth's temperature. But bison can only do their job as grassland caretakers and community builders if we protect them and their habitats.

Prairie crocuses starting to bloom.
ROBERT JOHNSON

Ryley with a bison in a squeeze chute. This "hugging machine" keeps bison still and safe while they are checked and weighed.
ROBERT JOHNSON

Reid displays a freshly dug timpsila root and a mature timpsila plant stem with dried-out leaves and flowers.
ROBERT JOHNSON

GROWING UP WITH BISON

What's it like to grow up with bison? I posed that question to 14-year-old Ryley, 11-year-old Reid, 10-year-old Rhett and 9-year-old Rory. Their parents, Robert and Rebecca Johnson, have been raising bison on RJ Game Farm in southeastern Saskatchewan since 2007. The kids have spent their whole lives there.

There are usually 2,000 bison on the farm. They live outside year-round but get extra food in winter. On weekends and after school, the kids take turns helping their parents deliver hay to the bison. They hop in and out of the tractor cab to open and close gates. They also unwrap bales. In the fall Rory collects fallen apples and hauls them to the pastures with her mom as a treat for the bison. In spring the kids often go with their parents to look for newborn calves.

Ryley does several important jobs when the bison are brought into the barn for their yearly weighing, checkup and shots. She fills needles with vaccine and occasionally gives injections. She also prepares ear tags and enters data into the computer.

But there's more to life on the farm than chores. For Ryley and Rory, it's a great place for horseback riding—though never in pastures

From left to right: Rhett, Rory, Reid and Ryley sit on a snowbank with their dog, Smokey.
ROBERT JOHNSON

where there are bison. Rhett likes flying a drone with his dad to shoot aerial videos of the herd. Reid enjoys all the plants and bugs he finds out in the pastures. The dung beetles are always interesting. And a few years ago he and his dad spotted a plant with blue flowers that they had never seen before. They did some research and found out that its English name is prairie turnip. They also learned that its roots are a traditional food for Indigenous Peoples such as the Lakota, who call it timpsila. Once the plant was ready for harvesting, they dug up some of the roots to try cooking and eating them. The delicious result tasted like spicy potatoes.

Other native grassland species, such as prairie crocuses, are also becoming more common now that bison are back on the land. "One thing I like about living here is it's not just the bison that you get to see," Ryley says. "It's the birds and the rabbits and all the other things."

> "ME AND MY DAD USUALLY WALK OUR DOG THROUGH THE PASTURE, AND I LIKE SEEING ALL THE DIFFERENT PLANTS, INSECTS AND BIRDS."
>
> —REID JOHNSON

A herd of bison gallops across the prairie in Custer State Park in South Dakota. Each year this park holds a roundup where visitors can watch people on horseback herd more than 1,300 bison into corrals for checkups and sorting.

PRISMA BY DUKAS PRESSEAGENTUR GMBH/ALAMY STOCK PHOTO

3
THUNDER AND SILENCE

INCREDIBLE NUMBERS

Before Europeans came to North America, this continent was home to about 170,000 wood bison and at least 30 million plains bison. About 2 to 4 million of those plains bison lived east of the Mississippi River. Most of the rest lived on the Great Plains. During the breeding season they gathered there in incredible numbers—sometimes tens of thousands. From a distance these herds made the grasslands look black. One Indigenous name for bison was inspired by their abundance. The Séliš and Qĺispé call them q̓ʷiq̓ʷáy, which means "many blacks."

European explorers and settlers were astonished by how many bison they came across on the Great Plains. They were especially amazed by the size of the summer herds. One traveler reported that he saw nothing but bison in every direction for three full days as he rode along the Santa Fe Trail. There was no way around them, so he just shoved through the

Long ago it was common to see bison herds on the Great Plains so dense that they blackened the land and filled the air with swirling dust.
MARCIA STRAUB/GETTY IMAGES

middle of the mob. Another man wrote about a similar experience in southern Saskatchewan. He said that the herd opened in front of his line of carts and closed behind them like water flowing around a ship, and the land trembled under the bison's hooves. Even when the big herds were out of sight, you could hear them plodding across the prairies. People said it sounded like the rumbling of distant thunder.

SHARING THE LAND

By the time the newcomers showed up, bison had been sharing the land with humans for tens of thousands of years. Some of these people lived in areas where the herds were small and scattered. Others lived on or near the Great Plains and were very familiar with the sight and sound of the thundering herds.

The plains bison's range is home to dozens of different Indigenous Peoples. Most relied heavily on bison for their survival from their earliest days and developed a strong spiritual relationship with them. For many of these Peoples, bison are more than animals—they are relatives. Each one has its own bison teachings, stories, songs and dances. They also have their own ceremonies and prayers to honor the bison and ensure successful hunts.

DELICIOUS AND NUTRITIOUS

When bison were plentiful, the people who hunted them on the Great Plains were among the tallest in the world because they had such a good diet. Bison were their main source of meat and fat. The brains, livers, intestines and other organs were also good eating. The blood made nutritious soups and puddings. And the tongues were a delicacy.

A single bison could feed a family for months. What they didn't eat right away they preserved for later. There were no fridges or freezers back then, so the women sliced the meat into thin strips and dried it over smoky fires or in the hot sun. If they wanted the dried meat to last longer, they pulverized it with a stone pounder and mixed it with bison fat. Often they also added crushed berries. When they packed the meat mixture into pouches made from bison hides, it would keep for months or even years. This food became commonly known as pemmican—a name that comes from the Cree word pimikan.

Aubrayla, who lives on the land of the Sicangu Lakota Oyate, helps butcher a bison harvested at Wolakota Buffalo Range with adults of the community. Many Indigenous people today are continuing and rebuilding their traditional relationships with bison.
JERRICA DONNELL

FROM TONGUE TO TAIL

Indigenous Peoples traditionally used almost every part of the bison they killed and tried not to ever waste anything. This showed their respect for the animals. It was also practical. Bison hunting wasn't easy, so they wanted to make the most of their efforts when they were successful. There are more than 140 traditional Indigenous uses for different bison body parts. Here are some of them:

HIDE: tipis, sweat lodge covers, clothing, moccasins, winter robes, bedding, pouches, straps, drums, shields, cradles, burial wrappings

HAIR: braided ropes, horse halters, bracelets, moccasin lining, doll stuffing

BONES: hide scrapers, knives, eating utensils, pipes, shovels, game dice, war clubs, sleds, toys

SKULL: ceremonial items

TENDONS (THE TOUGH BANDS THAT CONNECT MUSCLES TO BONES): bowstrings, arrow ties

Kansas settler Ada McColl gathers bison patties—also known as buffalo chips—for fuel in 1893.
KANSAS STATE HISTORICAL SOCIETY

FAT: grease for *tanning* hides, soap

BLOOD: paints

HORNS: drinking cups, ladles, headdresses, arrow points, medicines

HOOVES: glue, rattles, spoons

TEETH: ornaments

TONGUE (THE ROUGH SIDE): combs

STOMACH: cooking pots

STOMACH CONTENTS (PARTLY DIGESTED FOOD): medicines, paints

BLADDER: water containers, medicine bags

TAIL: knife coverings, whips, fly swatters

Bison also provided fuel for fires in places where trees were scarce. Well-dried bison dung burns well. And with every bison pooping 10 to 12 times a day, there was a lot of it lying around. If you were a kid in those days, one of your regular chores was collecting it.

Stoney Nakoda leader Tatanga Mani, or Walking Buffalo, wears a traditional bison-horn headdress. When he was born in 1870, almost no bison were left on the Great Plains. By the time he died, at 97, they were coming back.
GLOBE AND MAIL/LIBRARY AND ARCHIVES CANADA/DEPARTMENT OF INDIAN AFFAIRS AND NORTHERN DEVELOPMENT FONDS/E011307300

Two Indigenous hunters disguised by wolf hides sneak up on a bison herd. American artist George Catlin painted this scene in 1832 while traveling across the Great Plains.
SMITHSONIAN AMERICAN ART MUSEUM, GIFT OF MRS. JOSEPH HARRISON, JR., 1985.66.414/CC0

GETTING THE UPPER HAND

Imagine yourself as a bison hunter 1,000 years ago. Your quarry weighs at least 10 times more than you, and the top of its shoulder hump is higher than your head. You are armed with a spear or a bow and arrows. The bison has horns that can spill your guts onto the ground. If you have to flee, it will easily outrun you. I wouldn't stand a chance against a bison! But Indigenous hunters long ago came up with a variety of ways to get the upper hand. Some traditional hunting techniques were geared to certain seasons. Some were only possible in certain places. All of them required a lot of knowledge, skill, courage and planning.

One approach was to strike when it was hard for bison to get away or fight back. Experienced hunters knew where bison liked to cross rivers or lakes. In summer they waited at

Bison are good swimmers, but they are more at ease when they are on dry land.
ANDREANITA/GETTY IMAGES

This historical painting of a winter hunt shows how wearing snowshoes allowed Indigenous hunters to run on top of the snow while the bison had to plow through it. As the bison struggled to run away, the men could get close enough to spear them.
SMITHSONIAN AMERICAN ART MUSEUM, GIFT OF MRS. JOSEPH HARRISON, JR., 1985.66.416/CC0

these crossings and killed the bison as they swam to shore. When the lakes and rivers froze, they chased bison onto the ice, knowing that the animals' hard hooves would slip and slide on the smooth surface. Winter also gave hunters on snowshoes the opportunity to drive bison into deep snow drifts where they would flounder and become easier targets. In summer they could force the bison into marshy areas where they would get bogged down in the soft ground.

MASTERS OF DISGUISE

Another common traditional bison-hunting technique was to put on a disguise and sneak up on the herd. The hunter had to get close enough to throw a spear or shoot with a bow and arrows. He might have to crawl on his hands and knees across half a mile (0.8 kilometers) or more of hard ground to get there. Before setting off he would drape the pelt of a wolf, coyote, pronghorn, deer or elk over his body. The animal's head hid his own head and transformed him into a different creature. He might also rub his skin with animal fat and sage to mask his smell.

The pounding hooves of a stampeding herd of bison churn up the dirt and raise clouds of dust.
JOHANE JANELLE

The disguised hunter didn't just look like the animal whose pelt he wore. He moved and behaved like that animal, based on a lifetime of observation. Sometimes he might pause and sniff the air, or lower his head as if he were grazing. He knew the bison would take off if they sensed a human nearby but would not be bothered by a nonhuman animal. Bison will even tolerate wolves hanging around if they aren't acting aggressively.

LURING THE HERD

On the Great Plains, the Siksikaitsitapi, Cree, A'aninin, Cheyenne and others also used disguises to lure herds of bison to places where many could be killed at once. Even within one Nation there were different ways to do this kind of hunting, but it often involved donning bison hides. The young men who carried out this highly skilled and dangerous job were known as buffalo runners. Sometimes they wore a calf hide and bleated like a lost calf so worried mothers would come and investigate. Other times they hunched under the heavy weight of an adult hide—with the horns still attached to the head—and bellowed to get the herd's attention. As their trickery drew the curious bison closer, the runners kept

moving away. Slowly and patiently they led the unsuspecting herd toward a carefully planned route called a drive lane.

A drive lane was like a funnel. The herd entered it at the wide end and was guided forward by the runners. Other members of the community were spaced out along either side of the drive lane to make sure the bison didn't veer off track. At first the runners moved at the bison's normal walking speed. Then, as the herd got closer to the narrow end of the funnel, they broke into a run. If all went well, the bison followed their example and charged after them. At the same time, the people stationed along the route started shouting, waving their arms and flapping robes to keep the bison in the drive lane. Other people closed in from behind to frighten the herd forward. Suddenly the bison were stampeding straight toward their destruction. At the end of the drive lane was either a buffalo pound or a buffalo jump.

POUNDS AND JUMPS

A buffalo pound was a large circular corral made from tree trunks and branches, with an opening on one side. As soon as the bison entered the pound, people waiting nearby blocked the opening with logs. The bison could have busted

BUREAU OF LAND MANAGEMENT/
FLICKR.COM/CC BY 2.0

People have hunted bison in North America for at least 18,000 years. The oldest evidence we have so far is a stone tool with bison blood on it that archaeologists discovered a few years ago in southeastern Oregon. Ancient hunters used this kind of tool to scrape flesh from hides.

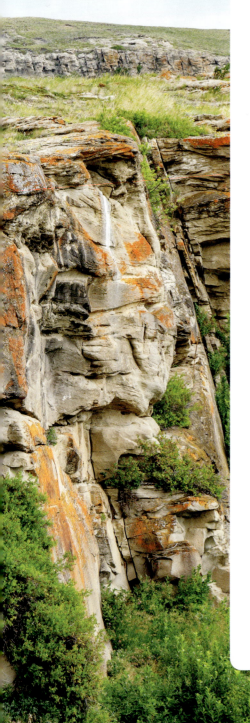

Head-Smashed-In Buffalo Jump in southern Alberta. This is one of the oldest and largest buffalo jumps in North America. Hunters first used it at least 5,700 years ago. The last time bison were driven over these cliffs was in the 1800s.
JEWHYTE/GETTY IMAGES

out, but usually they didn't because they were fooled into thinking the walls were solid. Bison hides hung over the walls covered any gaps where the trapped animals might see out. While they frantically ran in circles, seeking an exit point, the hunters picked them off.

A buffalo jump was a place where hunters drove bison over the edge of a cliff. The unlucky animals bounced off the rocks as they tumbled down. Or they soared through the air and smashed onto the ground below. The first to land were crushed by those that followed. Some died instantly. Others were only injured or stunned. Men waiting below the jump quickly moved in to kill any bison that survived the fall.

Buffalo pounds could only be built in places where there was a good supply of trees for construction. Buffalo jumps required land with features that helped guide the herd along the drive lane and ended with a steep drop. The best sites were used for thousands of years by generation after generation.

TEAMWORK

In many Great Plains Nations, including the Siksikaitsitapi, Cree, Nakoda, A'aninin and Apsáalooke, it wasn't just men who steered the herd toward a buffalo jump. Women and children also stood guard at stations along the drive lane and joined in the shouting and waving during the final stampede.

Women and children also often played an important role in buffalo-pound hunts carried out by Nations such as the Cree and Siksikaitsitapi. Sometimes they stood silently outside the pound, holding hides against the walls to make sure that not a single crack of light would show the bison a way out. At other times they clambered up the outside of the pen and yelled and waved from above to keep the bison from pressing against the walls and breaking them. Being that close to a bunch of panicked bison must have been both scary and exciting. Everyone knew that things occasionally went wrong and participants could be hurt or killed. But when it all went right, the rewards were incredible. Often more than 100 bison were slaughtered at once.

Successful hunts depended on many people working together to get the herd to the killing site. Then they had to work hard for weeks to butcher all the dead bison, preserve the meat that couldn't be eaten right away, tan hides and process other body parts. But during this time they also celebrated, feasted and enjoyed the company of friends and relatives they rarely saw. These big hunts usually happened only once a year because they took so much planning, teamwork and effort—and they usually provided enough food to last for months.

HUNTERS ON HORSEBACK

Bison had been fighting off predators armed with sharp teeth and claws for a long time before people appeared in North America. But their lives shifted as the two-legged hunters spread across the continent and developed new hunting tools and techniques. At first bison just had to dodge spears tipped with heavy stone points. Later the points got lighter, sharper and more deadly. Around 6,000 years ago the hunters figured out how to drive a whole herd over a cliff instead of just killing one bison at a time. And about 2,000 years ago, bows and arrows were added to the bison's worries.

An even bigger change came when the hunters started riding horses. The Spanish brought horses to North America

in the early 1500s. They tried to keep them out of the hands of Indigenous people. But within decades, the Pawnee and others had managed to capture some of these valuable animals. They were soon raising their own. During the 1600s, horses spread to Indigenous communities across western North America through trading, raiding and gifting.

Horses transformed these communities in many ways, including dramatic changes to how they hunted bison. Hunters traveling on horseback could go farther and faster when searching for herds. They could also match the bison's speed. A mounted hunter could race alongside a fleeing herd and target the best animals. Or a group of hunters could surround a herd and hold it in place while they made their kills.

MUSKET BALLS AND BULLETS

The introduction of guns to North America rocked the bison's world even more—but not immediately. The early models fired lead balls that often just bounced off the bison's tough hides. European settlers used them anyway. But most Indigenous bison hunters on the Great Plains stuck with their traditional weapons for years. They found bows and arrows more reliable than muskets and easier to use at a gallop.

When rifles came along in the mid-1800s, they were a game changer for everyone. The Sharps rifle was a particularly powerful and precise weapon that could kill a bison with a single bullet fired from a great distance away. Other members of the herd couldn't tell where the threat was coming from, so they often stayed put rather than running from the danger. Their confusion let the shooter keep felling them one by one.

54

THE BOOMING BISON TRADE

In the midst of the turmoil caused by the European invasion of North America, Indigenous Peoples who had always relied on bison continued to hunt them for their own needs. But fur traders and settler businessmen also wanted bison meat and hides. Both Indigenous and non-Indigenous hunters stepped up to supply them.

The fur trade created a massive demand for bison meat in what is now western Canada. When British and French fur traders moved into this area in the late 1700s, they had trouble finding enough food for themselves. Their problem was solved when they learned about a long-lasting, high-energy, lightweight Indigenous product made from bison meat. The Métis, Cree and others were soon producing enormous amounts of pemmican for their European trading partners.

European fur traders in the western United States had a different focus. They were most interested in hides with the hair left on, commonly known as buffalo robes. Indigenous people had been keeping themselves warm with buffalo robes for thousands of years. In the 1800s the robes became popular with settlers, who turned them into long coats, rugs, blankets and lap coverings for travel in open sleighs. Great Plains Nations such as the Lakota, Dakota, Kiowa, Cheyenne, Apsáalooke and Blackfeet played a large part in meeting the demand.

TRAINLOADS OF DESTRUCTION

Just as the deadly Sharps rifle was becoming popular, another threat to the plains bison arose. In the 1860s American railroad companies started laying the first train

People in historical costumes watch a young fur-trade reenactor paddle a bull boat at Grand Portage National Monument in Minnesota. People of the Mandan, Hidatsa and Arikara Nation taught European fur traders how to make bull boats by stretching a bison hide over a willow-wood frame.
GM SPOTO/NPS

Two men carrying rifles look at a bison that they have just killed.
NPS

tracks across the continent. The tracks cut straight through lands filled with bison. That was convenient for the companies because they had large crews to feed. They hired settlers to hunt the bison and provide fresh meat for the workers. William Cody was one of the best. In less than 18 months he killed 4,280 bison. That feat earned him the nickname Buffalo Bill.

Then it got worse. In the 1870s the new railroads brought trainloads of other white hunters to the Great Plains. Many were after only one thing—bison hides. Tanneries in Europe and the eastern United States had recently developed a new way of tanning these tough, thick hides. It was easier and cheaper than older methods. And, best of all, it produced strong leather that was outstanding for making belts to run factory machines. With new factories opening daily, bison hides were suddenly incredibly valuable.

The hide hunters killed bison as fast as they could, stripped off the skins and piled them onto eastbound trains. Occasionally they harvested the tongues and choice cuts of meat such as the shoulder-hump muscle. But they usually just left the carcasses to rot on the ground. In places the stench was overwhelming. Scavengers, insects and weather gradually cleaned the bones. Once they were bare, bone collectors loaded tons of them into boxcars to be shipped to faraway factories. There the bones were ground up to make fertilizer, gunpowder and glue, or burned to make charcoal for refining sugar.

KILLING FOR THE THRILL

The hide-hunting frenzy lasted just over a decade. During that short time, hide hunters massacred many millions of bison, quitting only when they couldn't find any more. They were to blame for most of the killing from the late 1860s to the early 1880s, but they didn't act alone. Trains crossing the American plains during this time often slowed down or stopped so passengers could shoot at bison just for the thrill of it. Railroad companies also organized special trips for large groups of sport hunters from the eastern states. Whenever the trains encountered bison herds, the hunters jumped up from their seats and let loose a barrage of bullets. Some fired from open windows. Others climbed onto the carriage roofs. Once they had downed every bison within shooting range, the trains chugged on.

Freshly killed bison and skinned carcasses sprawl across the snow in Montana in 1882.
COURTESY OF GLENBOW LIBRARY AND ARCHIVES COLLECTION, LIBRARIES AND CULTURAL RESOURCES DIGITAL COLLECTIONS, UNIVERSITY OF CALGARY/PUBLIC DOMAIN

SUPPORT FOR THE SLAUGHTER

The American government made no effort to stop the slaughter. In fact, it supported it. The government wanted to push Indigenous Peoples aside to make room for white settlers. Not surprisingly, the Indigenous Peoples did all they could to defend their right to stay on their ancestral lands and continue their traditional ways of life. The Oceti Sakowin,

> Between 1872 and 1874, trains carried an estimated 1.4 million bison hides, 6.7 million pounds (3 million kilograms) of bison meat and 32.4 million pounds (15 million kilograms) of bison bones from the Great Plains to factories in the east.

Cheyenne and others fought fierce battles against the United States Army. But the military commanders were determined to force all Indigenous people to move to areas reserved for them by the government. They decided the easiest way to achieve that goal on the plains was to take away the bison and starve the people into submission. The army didn't have enough manpower to eliminate so many animals all by itself. So the commanders encouraged the hide hunters and train-riding sport hunters to kill as many bison as possible. This cruel strategy caused Indigenous people great suffering.

The Canadian government also wanted to fill the west with settlers and knew bison were a major source of strength for Indigenous Peoples who opposed their plans. Canadian officials didn't do anything to stop overhunting until there were almost no bison left to hunt. Worse still, they took advantage of the sickness and starvation that set

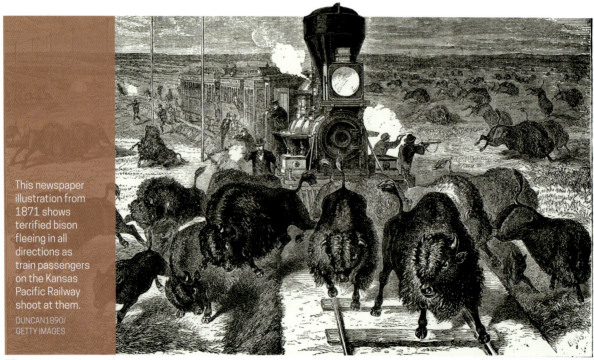

This newspaper illustration from 1871 shows terrified bison fleeing in all directions as train passengers on the Kansas Pacific Railway shoot at them.
DUNCAN1890/GETTY IMAGES

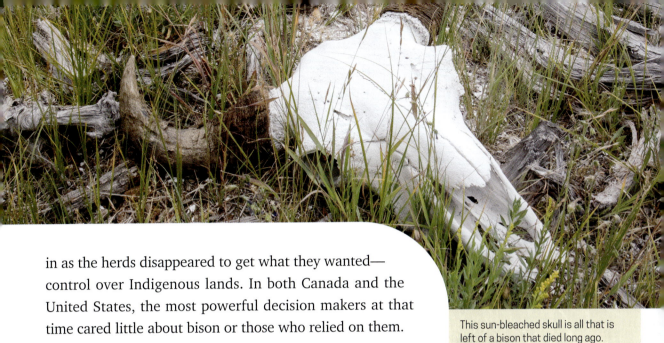

in as the herds disappeared to get what they wanted—control over Indigenous lands. In both Canada and the United States, the most powerful decision makers at that time cared little about bison or those who relied on them.

This sun-bleached skull is all that is left of a bison that died long ago.
JIM PEACO/NPS

NEARLY GONE

The destruction of bison east of the Mississippi River happened gradually. It started soon after Europeans arrived, and by the 1830s those herds were gone. But in 1865 there were still 10 to 15 million bison west of the Mississippi. Just 25 years later—in 1890—there were fewer than 300 plains bison left anywhere, and most of them were in captivity. The only free-roaming plains bison were in the United States. Wood bison were in just as much trouble. Only a few hundred remained in the wild in northern Canada.

The reckless slaughter of bison on the Great Plains got a lot of attention. Most people who witnessed or heard about it could hardly believe that the huge thundering herds could be wiped out and silenced. While many accepted the loss as the price of progress, others were horrified and alarmed. Some of them started trying to save this species. Thankfully, they succeeded.

If you could have taken the 30 million plains bison that once lived in North America and lined them up single file, they would have circled the equator 1.3 times. By 1890 a parade of the last wild plains bison would have been shorter than a city block.

JACOB W. FRANK/NPS

Wylee checks on bison meat drying over a smoky fire.
SHANNA WHITE

The White brothers, Jesse on the right and Wylee on the left.
SHANNA WHITE

LEARNING FROM THE ELDERS

Jesse and Wylee White live in Ronan, Montana, and are regulars at the Ronan rodeo. I met them when Jesse was 10 and Wylee was eight. They were already experienced competitors in the roping, bareback and saddle bronc events. Riding and working with horses is important to their whole family. This way of life connects them with their Blackfeet and Séliš ancestors who were expert equestrians—and especially skilled at hunting buffalo on horseback.

The buffalo slaughter in the 1800s was devastating for all Indigenous Peoples who relied on this species. But the buffalo and the buffalo hunters both survived this terrible time. Jesse and Wylee's daily bus ride to school takes them right past a wildlife preserve called the CSKT Bison Range. They see buffalo there almost every day.

They also told me about going on a buffalo hunt with their sx̣épeʔ or grandfather. This special occasion took place on a private ranch where buffalo harvesting is allowed, and only two buffalo were chosen to be killed. This kind of hunting is different from galloping across the plains pursuing herds that could run all day and never hit a fence. But it is always guided

Jesse and Wylee keep a lookout for bison as they ride through a field near the CSKT Bison Range.
SHANNA WHITE

by tradition. For example, after the hunters shoot a buffalo they offer prayers of thanks to the animal for giving its life so that they and their families can survive.

The brothers have learned a lot from their sx̣épeʔ and other Elders in their community. One teaching that has stuck with Jesse is "Don't kill too many, just how many you need." For Wylee, a key lesson is that every part of the buffalo is useful and nothing should be wasted. Both of them have learned how to cut buffalo meat into thin strips and cook it over a smoky fire to make a traditional food called dry meat. "That's one of our favorite snacks," Jesse told me. Wylee nodded and grinned.

> "WE CALL THEM BY THEIR SÉLIŠ NAME, Q̓ʷIQ̓ʷÁY."
>
> —JESSE WHITE

A herd of bison takes over the road in Yellowstone National Park, bringing cars to a standstill.
JACOB W. FRANK/NPS

4
HOMECOMING

ATATÍĆEʔ'S DREAM

Even when it seemed like there was no hope left for the bison, a few people refused to give up. One of the first rescue missions was led by members of the Séliš, Q̓lispé and Ksanka Nations, now known as the Confederated Salish and Kootenai Tribes, or CSKT for short. It started with a Q̓lispé man named Atatíćeʔ who wanted to create a protected bison herd on his people's lands in western Montana. That dream was eventually fulfilled by his son, Susep Łatatí. In the late 1870s, Łatatí traveled east across the mountains to the Q̓lispé's traditional bison-hunting grounds on the plains and brought home six calves. Under his care, the herd grew to about a dozen animals. Then his stepfather, Samuel Walking Coyote, sold them without Łatatí's permission.

Łatatí's only consolation was that the new owners, Michel Pablo and Charles Allard, were also members of the CSKT and kept the herd on

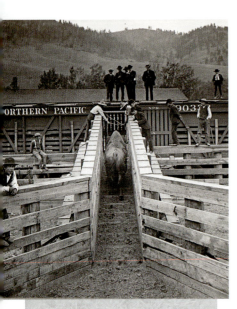

Cowboys coax one of Michel Pablo's bison onto the train that will transport the herd to its new home in Canada.
ST 001.036, MONTANA HISTORICAL SOCIETY RESEARCH CENTER PHOTOGRAPH ARCHIVES, HELENA, MT

the Flathead Reservation. There was lots of good grazing land and no fences, so the bison could wander wherever they pleased. After Allard died in 1896, his half of the herd was sold and moved away. But Pablo's half kept increasing.

FOUNDERS

In 1904 the American government carved up the Flathead Reservation and invited non-Indigenous people to come and settle there. The Séliš, Qĺispé and Ksanka were left with just a fraction of the lands that had been promised to them through a treaty signed many years earlier. By then Pablo had the world's largest herd of plains bison. But he no longer had enough room for them, so he had no choice but to sell his beloved animals. The Canadian government bought them.

Between 1907 and 1912, Pablo's 762 bison were rounded up, loaded into special train cars and shipped to Alberta. They were meant to be the star attraction in Canada's brand-new Buffalo National Park. But the park was plagued with problems, including widespread illness among its bison. In 1939 the park was closed, and the remaining animals were killed. Luckily, all was not lost.

On their way to Buffalo National Park, many of Pablo's bison stopped over in another Alberta park that is now called Elk Island National Park. About 50 stayed there and became the founders of a herd that has helped bring back bison all across the continent. To keep Elk Island from getting too crowded, its extra bison are sent to other parks, wildlife preserves and zoos. Some have even gone as far as South Africa, Australia and Great Britain. Today most of Canada's plains bison and many in the United States have family connections to the Elk Island National Park herd.

A newborn bison calf rests on the ground.
JACOB W. FRANK/NPS

TO THE RESCUE

The Flathead Reservation herd was one of five rescue herds that played a major role in keeping plains bison from going extinct. Like Atatíće? and those who followed his dream, the people who started these herds refused to give up on this species. Instead they took action to turn things around.

- James McKay, who was Métis, and Charles Alloway, who came to Canada from Ireland, hunted bison for years but quit after seeing how quickly the herds were disappearing. In 1873 and 1874 the two friends joined Métis buffalo-hunting brigades in hopes of saving some calves. They brought five back to McKay's Manitoba ranch and started Canada's first rescue herd.

A young bison calf peeks out from behind a clump of silvery sagebrush.
JANE GAMBLE/NPS

- In the early 1880s French Canadian rancher Frederick Dupuis and his Lakota wife, Good Elk Woman, caught a few calves during one of their last buffalo hunts. They took them back to South Dakota and ranged them with their cattle on the Cheyenne River Reservation. This herd grew to more than 900 animals before it was divided and sold off in the early 1900s. Thirty-six went to Custer State Park and launched its world-famous bison conservation program.

- Texas ranchers Mary Ann and Charles Goodnight began raising buffalo in 1878 after Mary Ann convinced her husband to save four calves from one of the last herds on the southern plains. He believed wild buffalo had to go to make way for settlers. But she hated the hide hunters' brutality and worried about the buffalo's future. Today the Goodnight herd carries on as the Texas State Bison Herd in Caprock Canyons State Park.

- Charles Jesse Jones, better known as Buffalo Jones, was a hotshot hide hunter in the 1870s. He killed thousands of buffalo but felt guilty about it. So in 1886 he began to make amends. Over four years he captured 66 calves—lassoing them or grabbing them by their tails—in Texas, Nebraska and Kansas. They multiplied on his Kansas ranch along with other buffalo he bought. Members of his herd were scattered across the continent as he sold them to other private owners.

MOO-VE OVER, BUFFALOS

Charles Goodnight and Buffalo Jones cared about their charges. But they also looked at them and saw dollar signs. They figured they could cross bison and domestic beef cattle and get a valuable new kind of animal. Bison have remarkable hardiness for surviving cold, snowy winters and hot, dry summers. Cattle excel at meat production. And their offspring—dubbed cattalo—would have the best features of both. At least, that was the theory. Goodnight and Jones spent years trying to come up with the perfect crossbreed before giving up on this experiment.

Others also dabbled in raising cattalo or accidentally ended up with crossbreeds because their cattle and bison lived together. Michel Pablo and Charles Allard were among the few who tried to keep their herd pure. In 1893 they bought 26 bison and 18 cattalo from Buffalo Jones. But they kept the cattalo on an island in the middle of a lake, well away from their bison. Eventually others who were working to save this species also realized that crossbreeding was bad for bison and put a stop to it.

For years bison experts thought that there were still a handful of purebred herds around, in places like Elk Island National Park and Yellowstone National Park. But research with new technology shows that most modern bison have one or more cattalo ancestors. Fortunately, having a smidgeon of cattle *DNA* doesn't really seem to affect the way a bison looks or behaves.

Experimental crossbreeding between bison and beef cattle produced some strange-looking animals—like this cattalo bull that lived in Buffalo National Park in the early 1900s. But bison that have only a tiny amount of cattle DNA look almost identical to purebred bison.
FRANK W. BELL/PUBLIC DOMAIN

STUFFED, MOUNTED AND CAGED

In 1886—the same year Buffalo Jones started his rescue operation—William Hornaday shot 21 of the last bison in Montana. Among them were the biggest bull his hunting companions had ever seen and a calf that was only months old. Oddly, his reason for killing these animals was that he wanted to save their species. Hornaday was the chief taxidermist for the United States National Museum in Washington, DC. A taxidermist is someone who stuffs and mounts the skins of dead animals to create lifelike displays.

When William Hornaday's bison exhibit opened to the public in March 1888, it was a huge hit. Museum visitors could walk around the glass case and examine the stuffed and mounted bison from all angles.
SMITHSONIAN INSTITUTION ARCHIVES/CC0

Using six of the bison he had killed, Hornaday set out to show how magnificent these animals were. He hoped his display would inspire museum visitors to help protect the few remaining bison.

Hornaday's next project was bringing live bison to New York City. The Bronx Zoo opened in 1899 with him in charge and soon had bison on show. Again he wanted people who saw them to care about this species, but he also had other plans for the herd. In 1905 Hornaday rounded up some friends and started the American Bison Society. They weren't satisfied with simply safeguarding bison in zoos and on private ranches. They wanted to return them to wide open spaces on public lands.

A group of children and their teacher curiously examine the first bison at the National Zoological Park in Washington, DC, in 1899.
SMITHSONIAN INSTITUTION ARCHIVES/CC0

THE DARK SIDE OF SUCCESS

In October 1907 the American Bison Society organized the shipment of 15 Bronx Zoo bison to the Wichita National Forest and Game Preserve in Oklahoma. Their release onto the spacious grasslands marked a turning point for bison conservation in the United States. Hornaday was widely hailed as a hero. But the dark side of this achievement was largely ignored. The Wichita preserve was on territory that the United States government had set aside for the Kiowa, Numunuu and Apache in 1867—and then snatched back from them in 1901.

In 1913, 14 more Bronx Zoo bison headed off to Wind Cave National Park in the Black Hills of South Dakota. It was another example of welcoming bison back to lands that had been taken from Indigenous Peoples by force.

Wind Cave is sacred to the Lakota as the site of their Emergence Story. This place—Maka Oníya or "breathing

American postage stamps, coins and paper money have all been adorned with bison modeled on the big bull in William Hornaday's museum display. The famous bull's image also appears on the badges worn by US National Park Service employees.

JOHN EICHER/NPS

earth"—is where the first bison herd and the first Lakota came up from underground. It is also where the Creator instructed the first people to follow the footprints of the bison, who would lead them to water and provide everything they needed to survive. In 1868 the United States government signed over the Black Hills to the Lakota. Eight years later the government broke its treaty promise, waged war against the Lakota and took possession of the Black Hills. The US military's support for the 1870s slaughter of wild bison had helped it win this territory. At the time no one could have imagined that it would one day be a sanctuary for zoo-raised bison and their descendants.

TEARS AND SMILES

The American Bison Society was also behind the creation of a protected area for bison that opened in 1909. The society

Today about 350 to 500 bison live in Wind Cave National Park. Since the park is fairly small, visitors have an excellent chance of seeing some of them.
MARK NEWMAN/GETTY IMAGES

persuaded the federal government to seize nearly 30 square miles (78 square kilometers) of land from the Flathead Reservation to set up the National Bison Range. It also raised money to buy the starter herd. Most of those bison came from the family that had bought Charles Allard's half of the Flathead Reservation herd after he died.

Their return was bittersweet for the Confederated Salish and Kootenai Tribes. First the government carved up the reservation and refused to buy Michel Pablo's bison when he was forced to sell them. Now it was taking away some of their best remaining hunting grounds to make a home for bison that they could have nothing to do with. For many decades Tribal members were officially barred from working on the National Bison Range.

The CSKT kept trying to regain control of these lands and finally succeeded in 2020. They took over full responsibility for the bison's care in 2022. Their three-day celebration included prayers, dances, songs, speeches, a few tears and many big smiles. Today the preserve is called the CSKT Bison Range or simply the Bison Range.

SURVIVORS IN THE WILD

By the time plains bison hit rock bottom, the only place this species remained in the wild was Yellowstone National Park. In the 1870s and 1880s there were still hundreds of bison in the Yellowstone area. The national park was created in 1872 to protect them, but illegal hunting continued until 1894. That's when the first US federal law that specifically protected bison was passed, and soldiers were sent to Yellowstone to enforce it.

I met this bison bull on the road as I was driving through the CSKT Bison Range. I stopped the car, took a picture through the front window and waited while he calmly detoured around me.
FRANCES BACKHOUSE

Unfortunately they couldn't do anything for the bison outside the park boundaries. By 1901 the only bison left in the Yellowstone area were about two dozen that were living safely inside the park.

In 1902 the park managers added 21 adult bison from two rescue herds. The new arrivals were put in a fenced pasture far from the wild herd. Once they settled in, they were allowed to roam in the summer. But each fall they were brought back to the park's Lamar Buffalo Ranch and fed hay until spring. In 1952 their winter vacations ended. They began fending for themselves year-round and mixing more often with the free-ranging herd. By 1954 there were about 1,300 bison living in various parts of the park.

WOOD BUFFALO WOES

Wood bison also hung on in only one location in the wild. Their last refuge was in an area that straddles the border between Alberta and the Northwest Territories. At their lowest point, around 1900, there were about 200 survivors. Like the United States, Canada didn't give bison legal protection until it was almost too late. The first effective Canadian

This area of Wood Buffalo National Park is called Sweetgrass because of its vast wet meadows. It is a favorite grazing area for bison. Wolves are also often present.
©J.D.MCKINNON/PARKS CANADA, WOOD BUFFALO NATIONAL PARK

bison protection law wasn't passed until 1894—15 years after the country's last wild plains bison was killed. But that law did help the remaining wood bison. So did the creation of Wood Buffalo National Park in 1922. By then there were about 1,500 wood bison living in the area.

Meanwhile, Buffalo National Park—the place that had taken in most of Pablo's herd when he had to sell it—was bursting at the seams. To ease the pressure, thousands of those plains bison were moved from there to Wood Buffalo National Park in the 1920s. The park managers weren't concerned about mixing plains bison in with wood bison because they didn't consider them different subspecies. They also planned to keep the two groups far apart so they would never meet or mate. But the bison had other ideas. They did meet and they did mate. Does it matter that most wood bison now have some distant plains bison ancestors? The answer depends on whom you ask. But everyone agrees that the other result of the transfer was disastrous. The Buffalo National Park bison carried two foreign diseases, bovine tuberculosis and brucellosis, to their new home. And wood bison have been paying the price for that blunder ever since.

DOUBLE WHAMMY

Bovine tuberculosis, or TB, and brucellosis did not exist in North America before Europeans brought domestic cattle to the continent. The cattle carried the bacteria that cause these diseases and passed them on to bison. Once bovine TB and brucellosis got into bison herds, they continued to spread. Stopping them was and still is tricky because some infected animals show no signs of illness. But others do get sick, and it can be fatal. Bison weakened by bovine

Theodore Roosevelt National Park staff examine a bison cow held in a squeeze chute. The park's bison are rounded up every few years for health checks. Some are sent to new homes to prevent overcrowding.
NPS

TB or brucellosis are easier targets for predators and have a harder time surviving the winter. Both diseases can also cause health problems that reduce the number of calves born in affected herds.

Bison in Wood Buffalo National Park and the surrounding area still carry bovine TB and brucellosis. Other wood bison don't. That's thanks to a small herd that stayed tucked away in a remote corner of the park until biologists found it in 1958. After five years of testing, 40 of these bison were declared disease-free. They were taken to two locations outside the park, far from the infected bison. Since then descendants of the disease-free animals have launched several new herds in northern Canada and Alaska.

About 3,000 bison currently live in Wood Buffalo National Park. This is the continent's largest herd of free-ranging wood bison. Unfortunately, they can't be moved from the park to build up herds in other places because they might bring bovine TB and brucellosis with them. They are also confined by a no-go zone set up to prevent them from contacting disease-free bison or cattle. These restrictions have significantly slowed down wood bison recovery efforts.

TROUBLE IN YELLOWSTONE

The only plains bison herds that still carry brucellosis live in and around Yellowstone National Park. This is a serious problem, because North American cattle no longer carry this disease and there are a lot of cattle ranches in that area. Yellowstone's bison sometimes wander out of the park, especially in the fall. They are drawn to the plains and valleys where their ancestors used to spend the winter. But that habitat has been taken over by people, including cattle ranchers who are afraid the bison will transmit brucellosis to their livestock. There's no record of this ever happening, but they don't want to take any chances.

Bison are most likely to leave the park when they feel crowded. For many years the only way park managers were able to keep the herds from getting too big was by regularly eliminating some of their members. They would have preferred to send the extra bison to places where they could help restore this species. But they couldn't risk sending brucellosis with them. So park staff captured some bison every year and trucked them to facilities where they were killed and butchered for meat. Hunters were also allowed to shoot bison that crossed the park boundaries. These measures are no longer the only solution. In 2018 Yellowstone National Park embarked on a new approach called the Bison Conservation Transfer Program. It captures some of the straying bison and tests them for brucellosis. If they are declared disease-free, they can go to new homes.

Bison mingle in a corral at a quarantine site just outside Yellowstone National Park. They were captured as part of Yellowstone's Bison Conservation and Transfer Program. From here they will be trucked to another quarantine facility on the Fort Peck Reservation.
JIM PEACO/NPS

RENEWING RELATIONSHIPS

The transfer program has already saved the lives of hundreds of bison. It is also supporting the return of bison to Indigenous communities across the United States. The captured animals have to be quarantined for up to three years while they are being tested for brucellosis. This long process starts in the park and ends on the Fort Peck Reservation of the Assiniboine and Sioux Tribes in northeastern Montana. When the testing is completed,

In 2016 the InterTribal Buffalo Council delivered 10 bison to the Wind River Reservation, home to the Eastern Shoshone and Northern Arapaho Tribes. Their herd now numbers over 100 bison. They hope to have thousands someday.

WIND RIVER TRIBAL BUFFALO INITIATIVE

some of the bison join the Fort Peck herd. The rest are shared out through the InterTribal Buffalo Council.

This organization is made up of about 80 tribes in 20 states. It helps members bring bison back to their lands so they can carry on their traditional relationships with them. Since 1992 the council has delivered more than 20,000 bison to more than 55 Tribal herds. These animals have come from national parks, wildlife refuges, nature preserves and private owners. Each homecoming is deeply meaningful to the communities that receive the bison. Some people say it feels like a part of themselves that was missing has been restored.

LOOK WHAT'S IN THAT WALLOW!

First Nations and Métis communities in Canada are also returning bison to their lands. And Indigenous Peoples on both sides of the Canada–United States border are cooperating on buffalo restoration through the Buffalo Treaty. This alliance began in 2014 when 13 Nations and Tribes came together to create the treaty. Many others have signed on since then.

One of the signing ceremonies was held at Wanuskewin Heritage Park in Saskatchewan. For thousands of years this was an important gathering place and bison-hunting site for Indigenous Peoples such as the Siksikaitsitapi, Cree, Nakoda, Dakota and Dene. In the winter of 2019, bison were returned to Wanuskewin. The next summer their wallowing uncovered an amazing link to the past. It was a ribstone—a large boulder engraved with parallel lines that represent a bison's ribs. Further searching unearthed the stone knife used to engrave the lines and three more stones with carved markings. Archaeologists believe these four special stones are around 1,000 to 1,200 years old and are linked to a buffalo jump called Newo Asiniak.

BISON BUSINESS

Bison have come a long way since the late 1800s. Back then they were teetering on the edge of extinction. Now there are about half a million bison in North America. That's a win worth applauding, but it only gets bison partway down the conservation trail. Few of today's bison live completely wild and free like their ancestors did. In fact, most are part of commercial herds and live on farms and ranches.

A commercial herd could also be called a business herd. The bison are mainly raised for meat, just like beef cattle. Some commercial herd owners also collect the hair that their bison shed. The soft woolly undercoat can be spun into yarn for knitting and weaving. Farmed bison that are given the right living conditions can help support the health of grassland ecosystems and boost biodiversity. But they can't deliver the full range of keystone benefits. For one thing,

One of the carved stones that was found at Wanuskewin Heritage Park. It was buried near steep cliffs that First Nations used as a buffalo jump for more than a thousand years.
WANUSKEWIN HERITAGE PARK

BHOFACK2/GETTY IMAGES

If you eat meat, bison is a healthy choice. Bison meat has less calories and fat than beef, and it provides more protein. It also contains more iron and vitamin B12 than beef, pork or chicken.

A snowmobile leads galloping wood bison across the frozen Innoko River to their new wilderness home. This herd's founders traveled from Elk Island National Park to Alaska by truck. On the last leg of their journey they were flown across the state in a huge airplane.
JOHANE JANELLE

people who are in the bison business don't want predators dining on their livestock.

PRESERVING AND PROTECTING

Bison can best fulfill their role as a keystone species when they are part of conservation herds. These are herds that are allowed to live as naturally as possible, and whose care is centered on preserving and protecting the species. There are currently only about 6,000 wood bison and 25,000 plains bison in conservation herds. Most live on public lands, Indigenous reserves or reservations or properties managed by conservation organizations.

Today's conservation herds occupy only a tiny fraction of the bison's original range. But their numbers and their reach keep expanding with milestones like these:

> - In 2009 bison were reintroduced to northern Mexico. There are now two conservation herds on nature reserves there.

- In 2014 the Nachusa Grasslands preserve in northern Illinois welcomed the first free-ranging bison to live east of the Mississippi River in almost 200 years.

- In 2015, 130 wood bison were released near the Innoko River in west-central Alaska. It had been more than a century since wood bison were last found in the wild in that state.

LETTING BISON BE BISON

Many conservation herds live in places where there is only enough room and food for a few hundred bison or less. Hardly any of these places have predators that help keep bison numbers in check. So the herd managers have to keep removing some of the bison. To avoid that problem, bison supporters are working to create more large herds on large pieces of land where there is little human activity. With large-scale bison conservation, people don't have to meddle so much and can just let bison be bison on their own terms.

One large-scale project that recently got underway is the Iinnii Initiative. It was started by the four Nations of the Siksikaitsitapi, or Blackfoot Confederacy—the Blackfeet in Montana and the Kainai, Piikani and Siksika in Alberta. Iinnii is the word for bison in Niitsí'powahsin, the Blackfoot language. These Nations are working to establish a herd that will range freely across Siksikaitsitapi territory on both sides of the Canada–United States border. The project's first 25 bison were released near Glacier National Park in 2023.

The Nachusa Grasslands preserve is one of the few remaining refuges for the Blanding's turtle. When bison wallows fill with rainwater, they provide valuable habitat for these endangered turtles.

BRIAN A WOLF/SHUTTERSTOCK.COM

SAFETY TIPS FOR BISON WATCHERS

These days there are many places to go where you can see bison at home on the range. If you have binoculars, bring them. Because the number one rule of bison watching is: Don't get too close! Remember, bison can move quickly and have sharp horns. They can easily toss a human of any size into the air. Bison aren't normally aggressive, but they can be dangerous when they feel like they or their calves are in danger. Bulls also get hot-tempered during the mating season. Follow these guidelines to stay safe around bison:

- Practice car courtesy. The safest way to view bison is from inside a vehicle. When bison are on the road with you, they always get the right of way. Drivers should never honk at, nudge or tailgate bison.

- Use your thumb. If you are on foot, stay at least 100 yards (91 meters) away from bison. You can judge the distance by stretching your arm out in front of your face and giving the bison a thumbs-up. Then close one eye and see if your thumb covers the bison. If it doesn't, you're too close. Back away slowly.

- Do not disturb. Be calm and quiet when observing bison. Don't run around. Never throw food (or anything else) at them. Keep your dog on a leash.

- Pay attention to body language. A bison that is agitated—and possibly about to charge—will tell you how it is feeling. It may stop whatever it's doing and look your way, or swing its head back

A warning sign in Yellowstone National Park. Bison injure more visitors to this park than any other animal, usually hurting at least one person every year. Most of these incidents happen when people get too close to the bison.
JACOB W. FRANK/NPS

This bison bull in Wind Cave National Park chose a good spot to remind people to leave it alone.
FRANCES BACKHOUSE

Two bison watchers keep a safe and respectful distance from the herd they are observing.
JANINE WALLER/NPS

and forth while staring at you. It also might paw the ground, hook the ground with its horns, snort loudly or raise its tail. These are all signs that you should move off and give the bison more space.

SALUTING BISON

In 2016 the bison became the national animal of the United States. It is also Manitoba's provincial animal and adorns the province's flag. Bison are a state animal in Kansas, Oklahoma and Wyoming. No matter where you live, you can salute bison and support them as they continue to walk the conservation trail. Here are a few ideas of how to do that:

- In the United States you can celebrate National Bison Day on the first Saturday in November or National Bison Month in July. Canada's National Bison Week begins on the second Sunday in July.

- Get to know bison better by spending time with a conservation herd. If you can't visit in person, some places have webcams that let you watch live action online.

- If you live within the bison's original range, explore how their history shows up on the local landscape and maps. Are there any rubbing stones, ancient wallows or buffalo jumps around? Are there nearby places named for buffalo or bison? Some—like Stamping Ground, Kentucky—might not be so obvious.

WISE WORDS

It's hard to picture what North America was like when 30 million bison lived here. It's easier to imagine what we would have lost if their numbers had hit zero. We would have lost an animal that is revered by Indigenous Peoples and gave life to their ancestors for tens of thousands of years. An animal that is loved and admired by many people of all backgrounds. A keystone species. A climate ally.

One of the places where bison have been reintroduced is the Wolakota Buffalo Range on the Sicangu Lakota Oyate's Rosebud Reservation in South Dakota. The first 100 were released in 2020. There are now more than 1,000. Wizipan Little Elk played a major role in bringing tatanka back to these lands. "They have always taken care of us and we need to take care of them," he says. That wisdom can guide all of us as we continue to restore our relationship with North America's largest land animal.

SWISSHIPPO/GETTY IMAGES

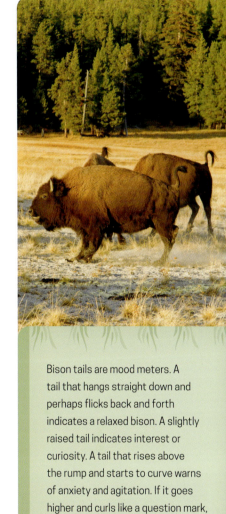

Bison tails are mood meters. A tail that hangs straight down and perhaps flicks back and forth indicates a relaxed bison. A slightly raised tail indicates interest or curiosity. A tail that rises above the rump and starts to curve warns of anxiety and agitation. If it goes higher and curls like a question mark, the bison is seriously upset.

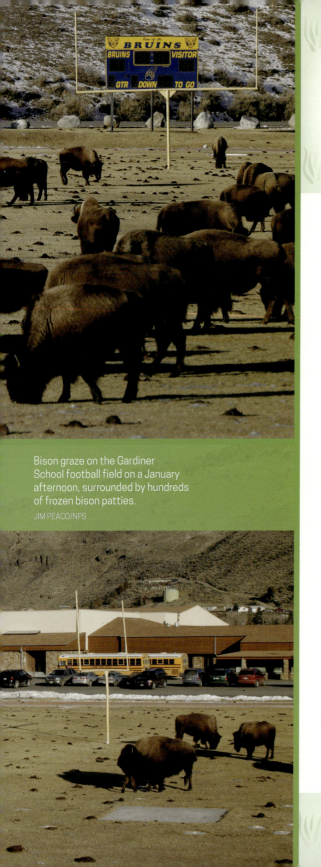

Bison graze on the Gardiner School football field on a January afternoon, surrounded by hundreds of frozen bison patties.
JIM PEACO/NPS

BISON ADVENTURES AT HOME AND SCHOOL

Nine-year-old Rocco Stahler's eyes sparkle as he tells me about his best bison-watching experience. "They were this close," he says, holding his thumb and finger so they almost touch. The only thing between Rocco and the bison was his bedroom window.

Rocco lives near Gardiner, Montana, on the edge of Yellowstone National Park. Bison visit his backyard every few weeks in winter and spring. When there's snow on the ground, they push it away with their heads to reach the grass. "And in spring they're our lawn mowers," he says. Rocco always enjoys watching the visitors. This time they decided to watch him. For about 10 minutes bison kept walking up to the window and peering in curiously. Rocco pressed his hand against the glass—almost touching their humongous heads—and stared back. "I remember looking at them and realizing how big they are," he says. "It's crazy."

Bison are also a regular part of Rocco's days at Gardiner School. They often graze—and poop—on the football field. Students who got detentions used to have to clean up the patties before games. When the bison are on the football field, you can step outside to

Rocco is happy to have spotted this bison bull during a fall day trip in Yellowstone National Park. He knows to stay well away from it as his dad takes a picture.
DANIEL STAHLER

look at them. But you have to stay inside if they stroll into the parking lot or onto the sidewalk. Even kids who are well acquainted with bison may find them distracting. "Sometimes if they're really close to the windows, we get to look at them," Rocco says. "But usually we try to not focus on them and do our work."

Rocco's parents are both park biologists whose jobs include studying the relationship between bison and wolves. He has gone on research trips with them a few times and once saw wolves attacking a herd. "When I was really young, I thought wolves were mean for killing bison," Rocco says. Now he understands that they keep herds healthy by removing old, sick and injured animals. He has also learned that bison benefit many other species. "They're important to our ecosystem," he says. "And they help make Yellowstone more wild and beautiful."

> "I THINK IT'S REALLY COOL THAT I'M A KID THAT GETS TO SEE BISON OUT IN OUR BACKYARD."
>
> —ROCCO STAHLER

GLOSSARY

biodiversity—the variety of all living things

carbon storage—a process in which plants store carbon when they absorb carbon dioxide from the atmosphere

conservation—the preservation and protection of single species or whole ecosystems

DNA—coded molecules found in every cell of every living thing to provide instructions for development, growth and reproduction. DNA stands for deoxyribonucleic acid.

ecosystem—a community of living things and the nonliving parts of their environment (such as water, soil and rocks), all linked together through nutrient cycles and energy flows

grasslands—wide open areas where the natural vegetation is mainly grasses and there are few or no trees

Great Plains—a vast area of grasslands that stretches from the Mississippi River to the Rocky Mountains and from the middle of Alberta and Saskatchewan to southern Texas

habitat—the place where a plant or animal makes its home and can get all the things it needs to survive, such as food, water and shelter

keystone species—an animal or plant that has a very large influence on the health and functioning of its ecosystem

larvae—the first life stage of insects after they hatch. Larvae are wingless and often wormlike.

microbes—living things that are so tiny they can be seen only with a microscope, such as bacteria and viruses

pronghorns—very speedy hoofed animals that live only in North America, mainly on the Great Plains. They are sometimes called pronghorn antelopes but are not true antelopes.

range—the entire area in which a species is found

ruminating—the act of bringing food back up from the stomach and chewing it again

scavengers—animals that get some or all of their food from eating dead animals

sedges—a large family of plants that grow in moist environments and have grasslike leaves with stems that are solid (rather than hollow) and usually triangular in cross section

species—a group of closely related organisms that have similar characteristics and can breed to produce offspring

subspecies—a subgroup within a species. Different subspecies within a species usually live apart from each other.

tanning—the process of treating an animal hide to produce flexible, long-lasting leather

wallow—a shallow circular or oval depression in the ground formed by bison repeatedly rolling around in the same place. Also the action of rolling around in the dirt.

RESOURCES

PRINT

Hirsch, Andy. *History Comics: The American Bison: The Buffalo's Survival Tale*. First Second, 2021.

Olson, Wes, and Johane Janelle. *The Ecological Buffalo: On the Trail of a Keystone Species*. University of Regina Press, 2022.

Patent, Dorothy. *Camas & Sage: A Story of Bison Life on the Prairie*. Mountain Press, 2016.

Silverthorne, Judith (as told by storyteller and Wisdom Keeper Ray Lavallee). *Honouring the Buffalo: A Plains Cree Legend*. Your Nickel's Worth Publishing, 2015.

VIDEO

Buffalo People Arts Institute—Buffalo Hide Tanning and Teachings: nccie.ca/story/buffalo-hide-tanning-and-teachings

Iinnii Initiative: The Return of the Buffalo: ipcaknowledgebasket.ca/iinnii-initiative-the-return-of-the-buffalo

Peigan Board of Education—Buffalo Jumps: piikani.ca/about/old-womans-and-head-smashed-in-buffalo-jumps

The Path Back: ipcaknowledgebasket.ca/the-path-back

ONLINE

All About Bison: allaboutbison.com

American Prairie: americanprairie.org

Buffalo Nations Grasslands Alliance: bngalliance.org

The Buffalo Treaty: buffalotreaty.com

Canadian Bison Association: canadianbison.ca

Canadian Light Source—Educational programming and resources: lightsource.ca/public/education1.php

Buffalo Bill Center of the West—Great Plains Indigenous Peoples and buffalo: centerofthewest.org/2020/11/19/diverse-cultures-of-the-northern-plains-indian-peoples

CSKT Bison Range: bisonrange.org

Head-Smashed-In Buffalo Jump World Heritage Site: headsmashedin.ca

Honouring the Buffalo: honouringthebuffalo.com

Interagency Bison Management Plan educational brochures: ibmp.info/bisoneducation.php

InterTribal Buffalo Council: itbcbuffalonation.org

National Bison Association: bisoncentral.com

National Bison Week: canadianbison.ca/bisonweek

National Park Service—Bison: nps.gov/subjects/bison/index.htm

The Nature Conservancy—Bison: nature.org/en-us/get-involved/how-to-help/animals-we-protect/american-bison

Parks Canada—Bison: parks.canada.ca/nature/science/autochtones-indigenous/bison

Wanuskewin Heritage Park: wanuskewin.com

Wildlife Conservation Society—Bison: wcs.org/our-work/species/bison

Wind River Tribal Buffalo Initiative: windriverbuffalo.org

Wolakota Buffalo Range: sicangu.co/wolakota

For other references and educational resources, visit the page for this book at orcabook.com.

Links to external resources are for personal and/or educational use only and are provided in good faith without any express or implied warranty. There is no guarantee given as to the accuracy or currency of any individual item. The author and publisher provide links as a service to readers. This does not imply any endorsement by the author or publisher of any of the content accessed through these links.

ACKNOWLEDGMENTS

This book was informed by the work of Indigenous Knowledge Keepers, historians, biologists, bison managers and others involved in past and ongoing bison conservation initiatives. For specific research assistance, I thank Jason Baldes, Shannon Clairmont, Angela De Sapio, Jerrica Donnell, Heather Doyle, Stephanie Gillin, Tj Heinert, Becky Lonardo, Andrew McDonald, Wes Olson, Tera Parks, Tracy Walker and Shanna White. I'm particularly indebted to bison expert Wes Olson for answering the many questions I posed to him and providing valuable feedback on my first draft. I also greatly appreciate the feedback I received from beta readers Stephanie Gillin and Emily Rohrlach.

My bison-sized thanks to the young people who shared their experiences with me: Kaleya Blackbird-Runns; Ryley, Reid, Rhett and Rory Johnson; Rocco Stahler; and Jesse and Wylee White. Connecting with them and hearing their stories was my favorite part of the book research. Big thanks also to the parents, teachers and others who helped me make the connections and have those conversations: Sherry Bellegarde, Stephanie Gillin, Robert Johnson, Tera Parks, Daniel and Erin Stahler, Tracy Walker and Shanna White. And a round of applause to all the photographers whose work graces these pages.

As always, I'm grateful to Andrew Wooldridge, Ruth Linka and everyone else who is part of the amazing Orca Books team—with extra-special thanks to Kirstie Hudson and Georgia Bradburne for all they do to make my books shine.

And many thanks to the friends and family members who support my writing in countless ways, including being patient with deadlines and other pressures and celebrating each new book. Number one among those supporters is my beloved partner, Mark Zuehlke.

INDEX

*Page numbers in **bold** indicate an image caption.*

African buffalo, 6
Alaska, herd, **78**, 79
Allard, Charles, 63–64, 67, 71
American Bison Society, 69, 70–71
American Prairie Nature Reserve, MT, 2
Asian water buffalo, 6

Banff National Park, AB, 1–2
behaviors: in breeding season, 16–19, **27**, 30, 43; defensive, 11–13; rubbing, 33–34; stampedes, **50**, 51–53; wallowing, 30–33, 86
biodiversity, 39, 77, 86
birds, 28, 34, 36–38
bison: crossbred with cattle, 67; and disease, 64, 73–74; importance of, 39, 77, 83; as symbol, **69**, 82
bison meat, 45, 53, 55, **60**, 77
bison patties, 29–30, **46**, 84
bison watching, 2–3, **71**, 81–83
Blackbird-Runs, Kaleya, 22–23
bones: industrial uses, 56–57, **58**; skulls, 18, 38, 46, **59**; structure, 20
breeding season, 16–19, **27**, 30, 43
Bronx Zoo, NYC, 69
buffalo, use of term, 6
buffalo birds, 36–37
Buffalo National Park, AB, 64, 73
burrowing owls, 28, 30

calves, 10–11, 13–14, **32**, 65–66
Canada: bison protection law, 72–73; and bison slaughter, 58–59; imposing of reserves, 58–59; purchase of bison, 64
Canada-US cross-border herds, 76–77, 79

Caprock Canyons State Park, 66
carbon storage, 39
cattalo, 67
cattle, 67, 73–75
characteristics: appearance, 8, 15, 20; grazing, 14–16, 20–21, 26–30; life span, 21; ruminating, 15, 86; size, 5–6; speed, 13
Cheyenne River Reservation, 66
Cody, William (Buffalo Bill), 56
communication: body language, 19, **83**; vocal, 13, **18**, 19
Confederated Salish and Kootenai Tribes (CSKT), 63–64, 71
conservation: and biodiversity, 39, 77, 86; and crossbreeding, 67; defined, 86; and diseases, 73–75; quarantine, 75–76
cowbirds, 36–37
coyotes, 12, **38**
craters. *See* wallows
Cree Nation, 50, 52, 76
CSKT Bison Range, 70–71
Custer State Park, SD, **42**, 66

diseases, 64, 73–75
dung beetles, 29
dust bathing. *See* wallows

ecosystems, 39, 86
Elk Island National Park, AB, 64, **78**
European: settlers, 43–44, **46**, 54; traders, 55–59
European bison, 6

farms and ranches, 40–41, 60–61, 77
female bison (cows), 5–6, **9**, 13, 16

Flathead Reservation, 63–64, 65, 71
Fort Peck Reservation, MT, 75–76

Goodnight, Charles, 66, 67
grasslands: conservation of, 39, 78–79; defined, 7, 86; and grazing, 14–16, 20–21, 26–30; native species, 41, 79; rubbing stones and posts, 33–34; wallows, 32–33, 79
Great Plains: and bison, **32**, 43–45; defined, 7, 86
grizzly bears, 11, 13
ground squirrels, 28, 30, 35
grouse, 28, 36
guns, 54

habitat, 7, 34, 39, **79**, 86
hair: about, 8, 9, 12, 19–20; uses, 46, 77; winter coat, 31, 34–35
Head-Smashed-In Buffalo Jump, AB, **52**
herd: defences, 11–13; defined, 11, 16; travel of, 19–21, 27
hides: appearance, 12, 23; bull boats, **55**; tanning, 56, 86; trade in, 56–57, 58; transportation of, 56; uses, 46, 55, 56
horn headdress, **47**
horns, 12, 13, 17–18, 38, 47
horses, 53–54, 60
humps, 8, 10, 20
hunting of bison: ancient tools, **51**; drive lanes, 50–51; horses and guns, 53–54; pounds and jumps, 51–53, 77; seasonal techniques, 48–49; sport, 57–59; teamwork, 52–53; for trade, 55–57; use of disguises, 48, 49–50; weapons, 48, 53

Iinnii Initiative, 79
Indigenous: bison research, 22–23; cross-border herds, 76–77, 79; culture, 23, 41, 45, 60–61, 69–70; dependence on bison, 45–47, 57–59; lands taken by force, 57–59, 64, 69–70; names for bison, 6, 43; tribal herds, 63–64, 75–76, 78–79; *See also* hunting of bison
insects, 29, 32, 36–37
InterTribal Buffalo Council, 76

jackrabbits, **33**
Johnson family, 40–41
Jones, Charles Jesse (Buffalo), 66, 67

keystone species: and biodiversity, 28, 39, 77–78; defined, 25–26, 86
Ksanka Nation, 63, 64

Lakota Nation, 69–70

male bison (bulls): fighting, 16–19, 30, 43; size, 5–6
McKay, James, 65
Mexico, herds, 78
microbes, 15–16, 86
museums, 68, 69

Nachusa Grasslands Preserve, IL, 79
Nakoda Nation, 22–23, **47**, 52, 76

Pablo, Michel, 63–64, 67, 71
parks and preserves, 78–80
pemmican, 45, 55
plains bison: appearance, 8–10, 16; population, 43, 59; range, 7; and wood bison, 73

plants: and bison, 26–27, 29–30, 32–33, 35; prairie crocuses, 11, **39**, 41; sedges, 14–15, 27, 86; timpsila (prairie turnip), **40**, 41
poop (patties), 29–30, **46**, 47
population: current, 77; decline, 59, 70, 73–75; historic, 7, 43–44
prairie crocuses, 11, **39**, 41
prairie dogs, 24, 25, 28, 30, 35
predators, 11–13, 28, 78, 79
pronghorns, 25, **26**, 33, 86

Qĺispé Nation, 43, 63, 64

ranches and farms, 40–41, 60–61, 77
reproduction: birth, 10–11; breeding season, 16–19, **27**, 30, 43
rescue herds, 63–66
research: projects, 22–23, 85; quarantine and testing, 75–76
resources, 82–83, 87
RJ Game Farm, SK, 40–41
Rosebud Reservation, SD, 83

scavengers, 37–38, 55, 86
sedges, 14–15, 27, 86
Séliš Nation, 43, 60, 63, 64
Siksikaitsitapi (Blackfoot Confederacy), 50, 52, 76, 79
species, 6, 73, 86
Stahler, Rocco, 84–85
stones, rubbing, 33–34, 83
stone tools and carvings, **51**, 76–77
subspecies, 7, 73, 86

Texas State Bison Herd, 66
Theodore Roosevelt National Park, ND, 2–3, **74**

toads, **28**, 32
tourism, 1–3, **71**, 81–83
trains, impact of, 55–57, 58
turtles, 32, **79**

United States: bison protection law, 71–72; and bison slaughter, 57–59, 70; lands taken by force, 57–59, 69; treaties, 64, 69–70
United States National Museum, 68, 69

wallows, 30–33, 79, 83, 86
Wanuskewin Heritage Park, SK, 76–77
White, Jesse and Wylee, 60–61
Wichita National Forest and Game Preserve, OK, 69
wildlife: birds, 28, 34, 36–38; and bison, 25–30, 32–38; insects, 29–30; scavengers, 37–38, 86; use of bison hair, 34–35; and wallows, 32–33, 79
Wind Cave National Park, SD, 69, **70**, **82**
Wind River Reservation, 76
Wolakota Buffalo Range, **45**, 83
wolves, 11, **12**, 13, 21, 85
wood bison: appearance, 8–10, 16; and plains bison, 73; population, 43, 59; range, 7
Wood Buffalo National Park, AB/NT, 72–73, 74

Yellowstone National Park, WY: about, 71–72, 74–75, **81**; living nearby, 84–85; photos, **4**, **12**, **26**, **62**

zoos, 64, 69, 70

MARK ZUEHLKE

FRANCES BACKHOUSE studied biology in university and worked as a park naturalist and biologist before becoming an environmental journalist and author. Her other Orca Wild series books include *Owls: Who Gives a Hoot?*, *Grizzly Bears: Guardians of the Wilderness* and *Beavers: Radical Rodents and Ecosystem Engineers*. She is also the award-winning author of six books for adults. She lives in Victoria, British Columbia.